W9-ACJ-536

ELITE SERIES

EDITOR: MARTIN WINDROW

Soldiers of the English Civil War (1): Infantry

Text by KEITH ROBERTS

Colour plates by ANGUS McBRIDE

OSPREY PUBLISHING LONDON

Published in 1989 by
Osprey Publishing Ltd
59 Grosvenor Street, London W1X 9DA
© Copyright 1989 Osprey Publishing Ltd

British Library Cataloguing in Publication Data
Roberts, Keith
   English Civil War armies.—(Elite series; 25).
   1. English civil war. Military forces
   I. Title   II. McBride, Angus   III. Series
   942.06'3

   ISBN 0-85045-903-6

Filmset in Great Britain
Printed through Bookbuilders Ltd, Hong Kong

Author's Note

This is the first of two books in the Osprey Elite series
dealing with the recruitment, organisation,
equipment, training and tactics of the soldiers who
fought in the English Civil War. The first describes
the origins of the military theory used by both sides,
and deals particularly with infantry regiments. The
second will cover cavalry, dragoons and artillery.

Artist's Note

Readers may care to note that the original paintings
from which the colour plates in this book were
prepared are available for private sale. All
reproduction copyright whatsoever is retained by the
publisher. All enquiries should be addressed to:
   Scorpio Gallery
   50 High Street,
   Battle,
   Sussex TN33 0EN
The publishers regret that they can enter into no
correspondence upon this matter.

Dedication

In memoriam Andrzej Roman Ciupha, 1954–1987.
   With thanks to Julia Wheelhouse for her help in
proof-reading my efforts.

Soldiers of the English Civil War (1): Infantry

The Military Revolution

By the 17th century the military achievements of the Classical world had long been admired by more modern European theorists who considered that with a good understanding of Classical writers such as Julius Frontinus or Claudius Aelianus the 'Art of War' could be revolutionised. Initially this fascination took the form of direct translations of Greek and Roman authors; but the next stage, of commentaries on their use in modern warfare, soon followed. The first of these was Niccolo Macchiavelli's *Libra della arte della guerra*, which was published in Florence in 1521 and soon translated from the Italian. The first English edition was printed by Peter Whitehorne in 1560.

A number of 16th century writers, such as Diego de Salazar and Giulio Ferretti, made similar if less politically callous attempts to re-introduce Classical strategy and tactics. Although read and discussed with interest these works failed to change radically the organisation of armies or the ways in which wars were fought. The reason for this failure was the absence of two crucial factors: a thorough understanding of the principles involved, and the constant pay necessary to maintain discipline and training.

It was the Dutch leader Maurice of Orange and his cousins William Louis and John, who successfully wedded Classical theories to the changed conditions and weapons of the 16th century. They achieved this through a combination of extensive reading of Classical military texts, and experimental wargames. For the latter, lead figures were used

An illustration from George Monk's *Observations on Military & Political Affairs* (1671)—an example of the combined use of infantry and cavalry. This was potentially a very effective style, but, if defeated, the cavalry could ride away while the deserted infantry were cut to pieces.

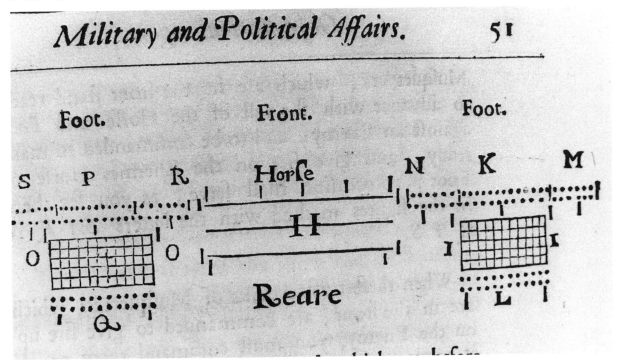

to discover solutions to the considerable practical problems which the process of re-learning Classical drill and tactics involved. The Dutch also had the necessary funds to keep an army in being long enough to train it in these new theories.

There were two key areas of change: the drill used to make units more responsive and manoeuvrable, and the more complex tactics which could be used by an army as a result. The new drill was taken particularly from the writings of Claudius Aelianus and used a standard system for five important aspects of drill: Distance, Facings, Doublings, Countermarches and Wheelings. The introduction of Countermarches was especially important in the development of firepower as it allowed the introduction of a system whereby each rank of musketeers fired in succession before retiring to the rear of the unit to reload. It would be wrong to suggest that the Dutch were alone in making military experiments; the Spanish, for example, had certainly been making some in volley firing. The advantage of Maurice's reforms, however, was the introduction of a complete integrated drill system for the Dutch army, something none of its contemporaries possessed.

The tactical styles introduced by Prince Maurice radically changed the face of the Dutch army with a re-organisation into smaller units termed 'battalians'. These were drawn up in a much shallower battle formation, ten ranks deep rather than the 40 or more found in the Tercios of their Spanish opponents. Perhaps the most far-reaching change was the tactical formation introduced for the army as a whole. Instead of the massive blocks of men used by the Spanish, Prince Maurice introduced a far more flexible system of triple battle lines based on the model of the Republican Roman *triplex acies*.

These reforms made the Dutch army a potentially more effective force. They certainly needed the advantage, since although the tactical style of the Tercios was basic in comparison with the Dutch battalions, the Spanish soldiers were veterans, and successful veterans at that. Prince Maurice was by no means a rash commander, and preferred manoeuvre and siegecraft to the risks of a pitched battle. The only major confrontation took place at Nieuport, the result of his reluctant but successful effort to relieve the siege of Ostend in 1600; but this battle was fought in such unusual

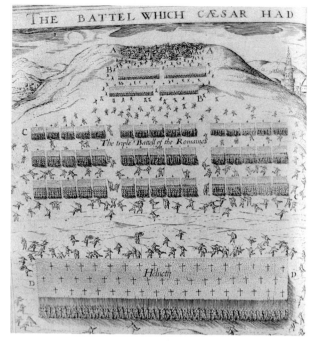

conditions that his success proved little for or against his new tactical style. It did show, however, that the new level of training and discipline Prince Maurice introduced had improved the standard of his soldiers.

Although there was no battlefield success to support his new theories, Prince Maurice's reforms caused contemporaries to reconsider the whole basis of their military thinking. The new Dutch practice was widely adopted in Protestant Europe, and the German princes sent representatives to John of Nassau's new military academy at Siegen. There was, perhaps, an excess of enthusiasm for the minutiae of the new drill; but the style of training inevitably produced more responsive soldiers and more manoeuvrable tactical units.

Catholic Europe remained unconvinced of the value of the new Dutch theories, particularly since the German princes who adopted them still fared dismally against the Tercios. Even so, Spanish military theorists saw the value of smaller units and by 1630 they had introduced shallower formations—although still not as shallow as the Dutch. The Tercios retained strongly offensive tactics but even in their reduced size their deep formations were still wasteful of manpower and lacked manoeuvrability. The Dutch style, on the other hand, made better use of firepower but was essentially defensive. The offensive quality of the

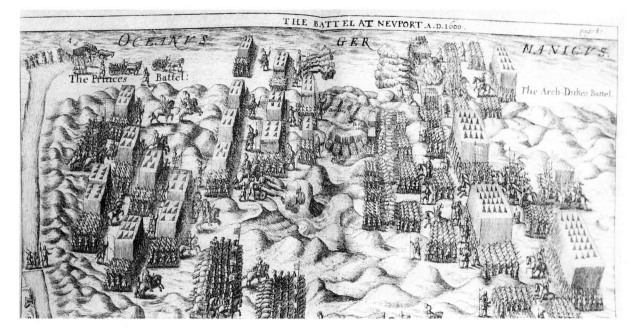

The new military styles introduced by the Dutch leader Maurice of Nassau, Prince of Orange were inspired by his extensive reading of Classical Roman and Greek texts. The illustrations here show the Roman *Triplex Acies* from a 17th century translation of Caesar's *Gallic Wars* (left); and a contemporary view of the Battle of Nieuport (right). This shows the Dutch 'Princes Battel' drawn up in the new style, and the Spanish Army in more massive but less manouevrable Tercios. (Author's collection, as are all other illustrations not otherwise credited.)

cavalry of both sides had deteriorated with their use of the pistol rather than the sword as a primary weapon.

The controversy remained undecided until the Protestant champion Gustavus Adolphus, King of Sweden, intervened to support the cause of the Protestant princes against the Catholic Habsburg emperor. Gustavus led an army whose organisation and tactics were based upon the new Dutch style, but which had been considerably developed by his own innovative ideas and his campagn experience in Eastern Europe. Gustavus introduced a new formation, the 'Swedish Brigade', a battle group of three or four mutually supporting squadrons. This formation required a still higher ratio of officers (both commissioned and non-commissioned) to men, higher levels of organisation and continuous training; but it was effective both offensively and defensively.

The chief tactical aim of the Swedish system was the combination of mobility, firepower and offensive action. The depth of infantry formations was reduced to six ranks, and these could be reduced still further for musketeers by bringing the rear three ranks alongside the front three and firing all together in a single great 'salvee'. This massive volley would be accompanied by the fire of the light artillery pieces Gustavus introduced, and would be immediately followed by an attack intended to destroy an opponent reeling from the shock.

Swedish cavalry were trained according to the same three principles. Most West European cavalry

A diagram from William Barriffe's manual *Military Discipline or the Young Artilleryman*. This shows a Company of Foot practising continuous fire; once the front line has fired it retires to the rear to reload, allowing the next rank to fire in its turn.

The Princes Battel:

relied on their pistols as a primary weapon and used the 'caracole' whereby each rank fired, then retired to reload. The Swedish charged home using their swords as the primary weapon and the pistol as secondary. This return to strongly offensive action was the result of Gustavus' campaign experience fighting Polish cavalry, and gave him a strong advantage until his opponents copied it. This advantage was increased by another innovation: the Swedish practice of mixing detached bodies of musketeers with cavalry squadrons to give fire support immediately before they charged.

Drill Masters and Drill Books

The English were introduced to the new Dutch style through their involvement as mercenaries or allies of the Dutch in their war of independence against Spain. One of the earliest works in this style to be printed in English was John Bingham's *The Tactiks of Aelian* in 1616. Bingham's comment in his introduction expressed the English view of the time: 'The practice of Aelian's precepts have long lien wrapped up in darkness, and buried (as it were) in the ruins of time, until it was revived, and restored to light not long since in the United Provinces of the Low-Countries, which Countries this day are the Schoole of war, whither the most Martiall spirits of Europe resort to lay down the apprenticeship of their service in Armes, and it was revived by the direction of that Heroicall Prince Maurice of Nassau, Prince of Orange'.

As an Appendix to his work Bingham added a copy of Prince Maurice's basic infantry instructions, *The Exercise of the English in the service of the high and mighty Lords, the Lords of the Estates of the United Provinces in the Low Countries*. This Dutch drill, indeed this actual manual, formed the basis of English drill from this time until the outbreak of the Civil War. It was used in 1623 as part of the new drill manual intended to turn the Trained Bands into a new and better 'Exact Militia' and can be found printed nearly verbatim in a manual printed for general publication in 1641 (*The Exercise of the Militia in the Kingdome of England*), as well as pamphlets printed for the King's Army in 1642 and 1643.

Several other English writers improved on Bingham's work with thorough guides to the new drill, Gervase Markham, Thomas Fisher, Henry Hexham and William Barriffe being the best known. These drill masters attempted to provide their readers with everything they needed to know about the military arts; and with the Thirty Years War spreading throughout Europe there was considerable interest in, and a considerable market for, their works. Some, such as William Barriffe, mentioned the new Swedish style, but English drill and military theory remained essentially Dutch. Most Englishmen seeking military service did so in the Dutch army or those of the Protestant German princes who followed Dutch styles.

Apart from military theory and the drilling of bodies of troops, the Dutch introduced one other important innovation: the illustrated guide to the 'Postures' used to handle musket, caliver and pike, fostered by John of Nassau but engraved and printed by Jacob de Gheyn. This was a very superior work of engraving in itself, which added to its impact; but it also served as the first standard system of small arms drill, and was soon copied across the whole of Western Europe.

The London Voluntary Associations

Military enthusiasm declined in London, as in the rest of the country, during the early years of the pacific James I, but was revived in 1610 as enthusiasts revitalised the voluntary 'Society of the Artillery Garden'. This was an association of some of the wealthier London citizens who met to practise weapon-handling and drill, sometimes with hired professional tuition. Although the citizens saw the intricate drill as much as a social accomplishment as military training, and some of their assemblies were distinctly theatrical, they were at least encouraged to practise. As the Society traditionally provided officers for the London Trained Bands, something of their enthusiasm was passed on to their men. The adjoining suburbs shared this enthusiasm for things military and formed rival associations—the 'Military Company' in the City of Westminster and the 'Martial Yard' in Southwark.

Some officers took this even further and formed

A closer view of Dutch infantry drawn up in three supporting lines. The Dutch military styles dominated English military thought at the outbreak of the Civil War.

Frontispiece from John Bingham's *Tactiks of Aelian* (1616). This shows Alexander the Great handing over his sword, and by implication, his military genius and pre-eminence, to Maurice of Nassau, Prince of Orange.

concession their neighbours must have appreciated at that hour.

Where the Privy Council's efforts failed to revitalise the Militia, fashion succeeded, and many country gentlemen came to London to practise with the voluntary associations, particularly the Society of the Artillery Garden. Sometimes these county enthusiasts formed associations in emulation of the London societies, examples being those formed in Colchester (1621), Bury St. Edmunds (1622), Bristol (1625), Great Yarmouth (1626), Ipswich (1629) and Nottingham (1629). Some prospered, such as the 'Artillery Yard' at Great Yarmouth, while others declined; but all looked to London for their inspiration. In the absence of an army it was the voluntary associations in London who were at the forefront of military theory in England, encouraging a wide market for works on military theory and providing a forum for discussion and experiment.

The Trained Bands

In the absence of any permanent units, other than a few garrison companies, the only military force in England was the Trained Bands. These Militia soldiers had their origins in the reign of Queen Elizabeth when the Crown realised that recent advances in military technology made it impossible for each man to own useful weapons. Apart from their expense, the new weapons required a higher degree of individual and unit training, and it was inconceivable that every man in the country could be trained in this way. The Trained Band soldiers were intended for national defence in time of war and to maintain civil order in peacetime, especially in towns and cities. For the latter duties in particular it was considered important that those enrolled 'must be men sufficient, of able and active bodies; none of the meaner sort, nor servants; but only such as be of the Gentrie, Free-holders, and good Farmers, or their sonnes, that are like to be resident'. The objective was to keep arms and military training in the hands of those with some stake in the country and away from the 'meaner

small groups dedicated to practising additional drill, examples being the 'Loving Gentlemen of Town-Ditch' and the 'Gentlemen of the Private and Loving Society of Cripplegate'. Captains Edward Ditchfield and Henry Saunders, who formed the group in Cripplegate, took this to extremes by summoning the men in their companies to drill every morning in summer at 6 o'clock: the captains claimed this provided 'no hindrance to men's more necessary callings, but rather calls them earlier to their business affairs'. Their soldiers 'neither beat drumme display Ensigne, nor discharge Musket: but only exercise their Postures, Motions and formes of Battell, with false fire in their pannes' at these early morning meetings—a

A page from the manual *Directions for Musters* (1638). This contains illustrations for the 'postures' of the musket (48) and the pike (36) together with elementary instructions for company training. The soldiers' costumes are copied partly from de Gheyn's original and partly from an English manual of 1623, so are not typical of the Civil War

Present.

33

Remoue yor right hand to the thumbe hole yor second finger to y.^e tricker with yor left hand fix the forke of y.^e Rest to yor musket and yor thumb against the forke, and the pike end of the rest on the ground.

Giue Fire

34

lift up yor right elbow and place the but end of yor musket within yor shoulder nere your breast, the small end appearing a little aboue youe shoulder standing w.th ye left leg foremost and the knee bent and the right leg standing stiffe

Dismount yor Musket.

35

Bring your musket and rest to your right side and carry both in the left hand onely

Vncoke your Match.

36

Take the match from the cocke w.th the thumb and second finger of y.^r right hand holding the musket and rest in the left hand onely.

Above: **Trained Band officers. These sketches are from engravings c.1635 on the brass clasps of the Great Vellum Book of the Honourable Artillery Company. The upper two are commision officers, the lower pair, a sergeant and an ensign.**

sort' who might turn their weapons on the wrong people.

As to the arming of these soldiers, 'every Captain is to charge Armes in his respective hundred or precinct, equally and impartially, according to the value of each man's lands or means, whether the owners be there resident or not. And no Armes are to be allowed of but compleat ones, and of the best modern fashion'. The Crown required a certain number of men from the county; the Lord Lieutenant of the county gave the task to one of his Deputy Lieutenants who would divide the responsibility within the county; and local officials finally made a fair assessment. This was a theory open to a good deal of abuse where friends were favoured with lower assessments and enemies or those who offered too small a bribe found themselves over-assessed.

Command of the Trained Bands was given to men of local influence and the position carried considerable prestige. This had advantages when it

The *Places of Dignity* in Rank and File. These places of dignity or positions of seniority in the file were important in a tactical sense, with experienced men in key positions, and the less experienced between them. With the exception of the two flanking soldiers—usually corporals—the places of dignity in rank were less important. The chart shows the seniority for files ten, eight or six deep.

The Places of Dignity of 10. in Rank.

| 2 | 6 | 0 | 7 | 3 | 4 | 8 | 9 | 5 | 1 |

The Places of Dignity of 8. in Rank.

| 2 | 6 | 7 | 3 | 4 | 8 | 5 | 1 |

Places of dignity of 6 in Rank

| 2 | 6 | 3 | 4 | 5 |

Rules of Dignity ought not to be regulated by ill cuftemes, conceived opinions, and falfe grounds; but by truth and reafon,

The places of dignity of 10. in File.

5	5
5	9
4	8
3	4
7	2
10	7
6	10
2	6
	2

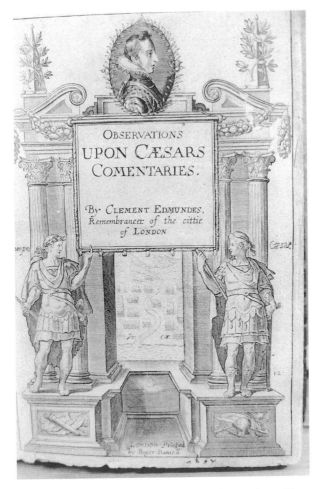

Frontispiece of Clement Edmonds' *Observations Upon Caesar's Commentaries*. This included as an appendix one of the earliest versions of the new Dutch style of drill published in English. The image above the title is Henry, Prince of Wales, the ill-fated elder brother of Charles I.

could only be combined at General Musters for training in fighting formations. The level of confusion on such occasions can be imagined.

The equipment of the Trained Bands was the same as that of the regular soldiers, which will be described later; but it was often defective, even ancient, as the citizens charged with providing it tried to do so as cheaply as possible. Another common practice was to exchange arms, that is to borrow them for a Muster from a friend whose company was to be inspected on a different day. Muster Masters tried to deal with this by having arms marked with a distinctive company sign, but the practice continued.

Experimental equipment: frontispiece of William Neade's *The Double-armed Man*. The author was an archery enthusiast who hoped to combine the offensive qualities of the bow with the defensive of the pike. It was popular with military theorists, but was never used on active service.

came to drawing men together for training, particularly in areas where a man from the next county was a stranger to be viewed with suspicion, but it also meant that few commanders had any military experience. The Crown made attempts to overcome this by introducing Muster Masters, professional soldiers who would inspect the soldiers' arms, assist in their training and report on their state of readiness. This met with varying degrees of success, as the county might refuse to pay too zealous a Muster Master while a lax one might be paid, popular but ineffective.

In theory the Trained Bands were to be trained regularly in small bodies and brought together once every three years or so for a General Muster of the County. City companies could be mustered together easily, but in the counties the companies

In general there was a great deal of inertia in the Trained Bands, and it took a national emergency or very enthusiastic officers to overcome it. The Crown made a significant attempt in 1623 to revitalise it and form a perfect or 'Exact Militia'. A new drill manual—*Instructions for Musters and Armes, And the use thereof: By order from the Lords of His Majesties most Honourable Privy Counsayle*—was produced and circulated, but the influence of the voluntary associations in London had greater effect, and this only because military exercises became fashionable.

The Trained Bands in the Civil War

The support of the Trained Bands may have seemed a doubtful advantage; but as relations between king and Parliament worsened both sides were conscious that they were the only formed bodies of armed men in the country. Control of the Militia, and particularly the appointment of their officers, became a critical issue as both sides hoped to use these soldiers as the basis of new armies. These arguments reckoned without the feelings of the Trained Bandsmen themselves as local interest, or self-interest, outweighed support for king or Parliament. King Charles appealed for the support of the Trained Bands when he raised his standard at Nottingham but, finding that they refused to serve outside the county, made the fateful decision to disarm them instead, a practice he then continued in other counties. Clarendon claimed this was done with 'wariness and caution', but in fact it was regarded with grave suspicion and lent credence to Parliament propaganda that the king aimed to disarm true Protestant Englishmen on the eve of invasion from Ireland. In fact Parliament also seized Trained Band arsenals but enjoyed more sympathetic press reports.

Trained Band soldiers did serve during the Civil War, sometimes forcibly impressed in field armies, but more usually in defence of their county or, particularly, in the defence of their homes during sieges of their towns or cities. In general, whoever controlled the county or the town could call out the Trained Bands if it was felt to be worth the trouble. Only two groups made a significant impact on the Civil War itself: the Cornish for the king, and the London Trained Bands for Parliament. The Cornish did so through sheer tenacity, but even they would not serve outside county boundaries. London was a special case.

The London Trained Bands.
At the beginning of 1642 the Trained Bands of the City of London consisted of four regiments totalling 6,000 men, half being musketeers and half pikemen. On 12 February a re-organisation was authorised to increase the total to 8,000, organised in 40 companies of 200 men each. These new companies were divided amongst six regiments known as the Red, White, Yellow, Blue, Green and Orange Trained Bands after the colour of their ensigns. The first four regiments had seven companies each and the last two only six. The following year the City of London together with the City of Westminster, the Borough of Southwark and the Tower Hamlets were surrounded by a series of earthworks

A file of pikemen from John Bingham's *The Tactiks of Aelian*, showing how the pikeheads of several ranks could project past the file leader to face the enemy. A depth of 16 men is shown, rather than the ten normal in 1616, because it illustrates the style of a Macedonian phalanx as a model for modern war. The figures are dressed as 17th century pikemen.

	White Regiment City of London	Yellow Regiment City of London	Green Regiment City of London
Musketeers	600	506	503
Pikemen	520	448	297
Officers	about 70	about 70	about 70
Total	1,190	1,024	863

	Orange Regiment City of London	Tower Hamlets Trained Bands	City of Westminster Trained Bands
Musketeers	630	819	1,084
Pikemen	408	385	854
Officers	about 63	about 70	about 80
Total	1,101	1,304	2,018

	Borough of Southwark Trained Bands
Musketeers	868
Pikemen	456
Officers	about 70
Total	1,394

William Levett, who compiled this report, estimated the strength of the Auxiliary Regiments of the City and suburbs at 1,000 men each. The only exception was The Green Auxiliaries with a strength of 1,200.

interspersed with small forts, the 'Lines of Communication'. Once these were completed, the six Trained Band regiments of London, three from the suburbs enclosed by the defences, and nine 'Auxiliary' regiments raised in addition (six from London and one from each of the suburbs) were brought under one authority, the Committee for London Militia.

Although the officers of these new regiments were picked with an eye to their political reliability as well as their military capacity, the real basis of these soldiers' loyalties was to their families and their homes, not the Parliament cause. They supported the Earl of Essex to oppose the king's march on London after Edgehill in literal self-defence. Their commander Philip Skippon's famous exhortation— 'Come my Boys, my brave Boys, let us pray heartily and fight heartily, I will run the same fortunes and hazards with you, remember the Cause is for God; and for the defence of your selves, your wives, and children: Come my honest brave boys pray heartily and God will bless us'—probably meant more to them than any political slogan.

Once committed the citizens were persuaded the following year to contribute 5,000 men to march with Essex's army to the relief of Gloucester, on the principle that it was better to defend London by fighting away from home than on their own doorsteps. Thereafter London and its suburbs provided brigades of infantry for service with the armies of the Earl of Essex, Sir William Waller and Richard Browne. This assistance was critically important, as in 1643 and 1644 the southern Parliamentary armies lacked enough infantry to take the field without brigades of City infantry. With the creation of the New Model Army their support was no longer so necessary, and no new brigades marched out of the City.

The Infantry of the Civil War: Organisation

As shown above English military theory followed the new Dutch style; this led the English to mirror the Dutch company and regimental organisation for their infantry units, but even so this offered a fair amount of latitude. The United Provinces attempted initially to standardise their companies, and in 1599 set a strength of 135 officers and men, these being a captain, a lieutenant, an ensign, two sergeants, three corporals, two drummers, a clerk, a chirurgeon, a provost, three pages, 45 pikemen, 30 musketeers and 44 calivermen. In 1609 the caliver was withdrawn from companies in Dutch service, and thereafter they consisted of approximately equal proportions of musketeers and pikemen. The reduction in the actual number of 'shot' was countered by the increased killing-power of the musket over the caliver, so contemporary opinion considered the actual effect on an opposing formation to be about the same.

The Dutch did not successfully achieve standards for company or regimental strengths, as the drill manual for English troops in Dutch service shows: 'Companies are compacted into Regiments com-

---

Structure of a Regiment in the Earl of Essex's Army, 1642

Regimental Staff

Colonel	Chirurgeon (Surgeon)
Lieutenant-Colonel	Preacher
Sergeant-Major	Waggon-Master
Quartermaster	Drum Major
Provost Marshal	2 Chirurgeon's Mates

The Companies

Colonel's Company	*Lieutenant-Colonel's Company:*
Colonel (as Captain)	Lieutenant-Colonel (as Captain)
Captain Lieutenant	Lieutenant
Ensign	Ensign
3 Sergeants	2 Sergeants
3 Corporals	3 Corporals
2 Drummers	2 Drummers
200 Soldiers	160 Soldiers

Sergeant-Major's Company:	*Seven Captain's Companies each:*
Sergeant-Major (as Captain)	Captain
Lieutenant	Lieutenant
Ensign	Ensign
2 Sergeants	2 Sergeants
3 Corporals	3 Corporals
2 Drummers	2 Drummers
140 Soldiers	100 Soldiers

The colonel, lieutenant-colonel and sergeant-major appear on the roll twice, as staff officers and as captains of companies. They also drew pay and allowances in both roles.

---

manded by Coronells. Regiments conteine not alwaies a like number of Companies, some having 10, some 11, 12, 13, 14, 15 and some thirty Companies and above . . . the Companies are some more in number and some lesse. Some reach 300 men, some 200, some 100, some 90, some 80, some 70'. This flexible system was still the norm in the service of the United Provinces in the 1630s, as Henry Hexham's manual indicates. Hexham refers to companies of 120, 150, 200 and 250 men, and uses companies of 80 or 160 men in his diagrams of company formations.

This basic model was followed in England, where infantry were formed into regiments composed of a staff and several companies. One essential difference was the absence of a standing army, which meant regiments were raised anew for each military expedition. This allowed the Privy Council or the commander it appointed to specify the theoretical strength of the units it wanted each time an army was formed. As a result the organisation of regiments varied somewhat.

Two interesting examples are to be found in the papers of the army to be raised in 1620 to support the territorial claims of James I's daughter Elizabeth in the Palatinate, and of that actually raised for the first Bishops' War. The first had 13 companies to a regiment, the Colonel's Company of 192 men, and the other 12 companies with 144 men. The second had 12 companies, the Colonel's with 188 men, the Lieutenant Colonel's with 140, and the other ten companies with 105 men each. In each case the number quoted is for private soldiers only, the officers, both commissioned and non-commissioned, being counted separately.

Sometimes the choice of regimental organisation left room for innovative ideas, an example being the five regiments which were to have been raised in 1642 to suppress the Irish popular revolt. The theoretical organisation of these regiments was to be a thousand men divided amongst five companies, one of which was to have been equipped only with 'firelocks' (dog-lock or English-lock muskets) instead of matchlock muskets and pikes—this may have been intended as a concession to the Irish weather. In the event only one regiment reached Ireland, the others being re-formed for service in England for the Civil War.

At the outbreak of the Civil War both sides

inevitably shared a common military heritage and tradition. As far as infantry organisation is concerned, however, this left room for considerable variations, as the original Dutch model was very flexible and the English themselves had recently begun to experiment in different styles. The most popular style had become a regiment with ten companies and a total strength of 1,000 or 1,200 men plus officers. The companies could either be of 100 men each, giving a total of 1,000 men in the regiment; or organised on an unequal system, with the Colonel's Company consisting of 200 men, the Lieutenant Colonel's of 160, the Sergeant Major's of 140, and each of the other seven of 100 men, giving a total of 1,200 men.

The army raised by Parliament and commanded by the Earl of Essex is known to have used the system of unequal companies described above, as the lists of regiments and officers printed in 1642 specifically say so. Parliament reduced the number of companies in Essex's regiments in 1644 from ten to eight, but more to force the merger of weak companies than as an organisational experiment. In 1645 the system used at the outbreak of the war was retained, and the New Model Army was raised on the same basis as Essex's in 1642.

On the other hand the Scottish army hired by the English in 1642 to serve in Ireland used a theoretical system of ten companies of 100 men each plus officers. It is not known which of these systems was adopted by the King's Army as a formal specification is lacking; certainly a regiment of ten companies was the aim, but which of the two styles was favoured is unknown.

In many respects the theory went by the board anyway as some colonels, particularly on the Royalist side, never managed to recruit a full regiment. In other regiments, however, the colonel's local influence remained powerful, and he was able to raise extra companies or incorporate others from disbanded units into his own regiment. The Earl of Manchester, for example, had 19 companies in his own regiment; Sir Arthur Haselrige had 12 in his; and Sir William Brereton had 16 in his, including three of Dragoons and one of 'firelocks'.

Militia regiments, both Trained Bands and Auxiliaries, followed systems dictated by local conditions, but were still based on the model of a staff and several companies. The number of companies in a regiment varied, as did the number of men in a company. Before the Civil War Trained Band companies in the Cities of London and of Westminster numbered 300 men each plus officers. The City of Westminster retained this theoretical system throughout the war but the London Trained Bands were re-organised to equal companies of 200 men each in 1642. In the counties the intention seems to have been companies of about 100 men, but there were many local variations.

Officers

As mentioned above, the officer structure of an English infantry regiment was based upon the Dutch model, and that of the Earl of Essex's army in 1642 is shown in the associated chart. This shows a staff of a colonel, lieutenant-colonel, sergeant major, quartermaster, provost marshal, chirurgeon, two chirurgeon's mates, preacher, wagonmaster and drum major. The company officers were the company commander, either a staff officer or a captain, a lieutenant, an ensign, two sergeants (three in the Colonel's Company), three corporals and two drummers. The first three were commissioned officers, holding a written commission signed by their general, but the others were also called 'officers' in contemporary parlance as they held a position in the company.

Three other officers are found listed in some regiments during the Civil War. These are the 'gentlemen-at-arms', the clerk and the 'lanspassadoe'. The first is to be found on the company rolls of both armies, and his omission in Essex's list is surprising. This officer, who was termed 'captaine at armes' in the Scottish service, was responsible for the inspection of the company's arms and the storage of its immediate supply of gunpowder, bullets and matchcord. The clerk is often found on both the regimental and company strengths; his duty was to keep the company muster rolls and often to receive the soldiers' pay and sometimes to distribute it under his captain's orders. The lanspassadoe was another junior officer who ranked below the corporal and whose duty it was to assist him; this officer is only recorded on the rolls of the Eastern Association, although the position is mentioned in several military manuals before and after the Civil War.

Numbers

Whatever the theoretical organisation of a regiment its actual effective strength was another matter entirely. At the outbreak of the war popular or influential colonels on both sides could fill their companies; but the experience of war soon resulted in widespread desertion, while cold, rainy weather and poor clothing caused heavy losses through sickness. Any examination of the surviving muster rolls shows that the infantry in the marching armies of both sides suffered terribly and only constant recruitment could fill the gaps. Although both sides had a common experience, Parliament proved better able to organise the recruitment of its infantry. While still weak in comparison with theoretical strengths, Parliament regiments remained stronger than those of their opponents. Both sides made attempts in 1644 to re-model their armies by amalgamating weak regiments and saving the excessive costs of weak companies with almost complete officer cadres. Parliament succeeded with its New Model Army, but the King failed to overcome the entrenched interests of his colonels.

Ensigns

In the 17th century every company of a regiment of Foot carried its own flag which was known as an 'ensign' or 'colour'. They were made of painted silk and measured approximately 6½ foot square. The ensigns of a regiment commonly followed a system whereby each company could be identified by the number of regimental symbols it bore. Thomas Venn described the most common system: 'The Colonel's Colours in the first place is of a pure and clean colour, without any mixture. The Lieutenant-Colonel's only with St George's Armes in the upper corner next the staff, the Major's the same, but in the lower and outermost corner with a little stream blazant, and every Captain with St George's Armes alone, but with so many spots or several devices as pertain to the dignity of their respective places'. A common variant on this theme was for the sergeant major's ensign to bear one of the regimental symbols instead of a stream blazant; this meant that the first captain would have two of the regimental symbols, and so on.

Although the system described by Venn was certainly the most common used by either side,

Regimental Strengths: Parliament Armies, 1644

Regiment	Date	No. of Men	Date	No. of Men
The Army of the Earl of Essex:				
Tyrell	April	297	June	524
Lord Robartes	April	363	June	700
Skippon	April	258	June	550
Fortescue	April	233	June	634
Barclay	April	?	June	475
Davies	April	196	June	316
Auxiliary Regiments with Sir William Waller:				
Borough of Southwark			April	611
Tower Hamlets			April	568
City of Westminster			May	604
The Army of the Earl of Manchester:				
Crawford	May	850	July	608
Pickering	May	738	July	524
Montagu	May	759	July	418
Russell	May	932	July	662

The King's Army: Reading Garrison: April 1644

Regiment	Men	Officers	No. of Companies
Thelwall	127	69	7
Owen	106	39	4
Lisle	189	81	8
Pennyman	360	119	11
Gilby	268	107	11
Lloyd	308	101	10
Hawkins	171	104	9
Stradling	246	105	10
Astley	146	71	8
Euer	59	32	3
Vaughan	195	65	5
Blackwell	56	30	4
Total:	2,231	923	90

These Muster Lists illustrate a major problem of the Royalist Armies—private soldiers melted away with disheartening regularity while the 'officer' cadre remains almost intact. At full strength the officers of these 90 companies would total 1,002, here there are still 923. The full complement of private soldiers would be 9,000 if each company had an establishment of 100, more if field officers had stronger companies, but there are only 2,231.

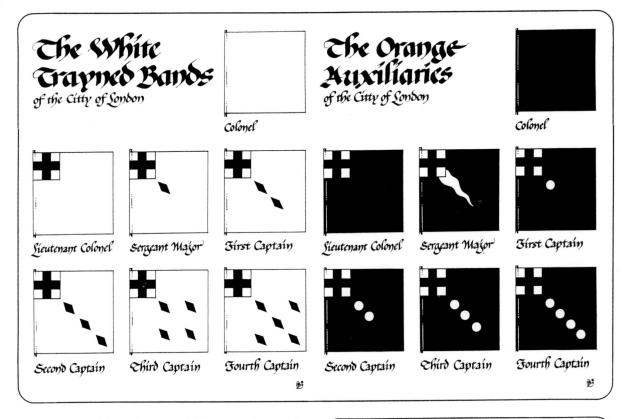

The White Trayned Bands
of the City of London

Colonel

Lieutenant Colonel

Sergeant Major

First Captain

Second Captain

Third Captain

Fourth Captain

The Orange Auxiliaries
of the City of London

Colonel

Lieutenant Colonel

Sergeant Major

First Captain

Second Captain

Third Captain

Fourth Captain

Every company of the regiment carried its own ensign, and the whole regiment followed a consistent pattern. Those of the White Trained Bands of the City of London were white with a red St George's cross in the upper corner; the regimental symbol was a red diamond. The Orange Auxiliaries of the City of London carried orange ensigns with white plates, but note in this regiment the sergeant major's ensign is distinguished by a 'stream blazant', not one of the regiment's symbols in this case. (Sketch by Dr L. Prince after contemporary ms)

there were others. The Tower Hamlets Trained Bands, for example, bore a central device on their red ensigns: the words 'IEHOVA PROVIDEBIT' between silver palm leaves in 1643, and a design showing the White Tower of London in 1647. Several Royalist regiments—the Duke of York's, Sir Allan Apsley's and Sir Charles Gerard's being examples—made use of a system whereby two colours alternated in triangular segments joining at the centre of the flag. The number of segments indicated the seniority of the captain: four for the first captain, six for the second, eight for the third and so on.

The colours chosen for ensigns were also intended

Ensigns of the Tower Hamlets Trained Bands, 1643. An unusual design with the words 'Iehova Providebit' in silver surrounded by silver palm leaves. The ensigns themselves are red, with silver plates along the top as company distinctions. (Sketch by Dr L. Prince, after contemporary ms)

The Trayned Bands
of the Tower Hamlets

Colonel

Lieutenant Colonel

Sergeant Major

First Captain

Second Captain

Third Captain

Fourth Captain

to relate to the particular virtues valued by the colonel who chose them. John Lucas in his manuscript *London in Arms Displayed* described the 'several complexiouns of military honour' as follows: 'Red: signifieth Justice or a noble and worthy anger in the defence of Religeon or the oppressed, White: signifieth Innocence or Puritie of Conscience, truth and an Upright Integritie without Blemish, Yellow: signifieth Honour or hight of Spirit, which being never separate from Virtue in all things is most jealous of Disgrace and may not endure the least shadow of Imputation, Blew: signifieth Faith, Constancie, Truth and Affection or Honourable Love, Greene: signifieth good Hope, or the accomplishment of Holy or Honourable actions, Orange: signifieth Merit or Disert and is a foe to ingratitude, Black: signifieth Wisdome and Sobriety, toogether with a sincere correction of too much ambition, Purple: signifieth Fortitude with Discretion, or a most true discharge of and Trust imposed'.

The 'colours' were the responsibility of an officer with the rank of ensign, the most junior of the three commissioned officers in a company. This officer carried them in action or parade but probably not on the march. The flag was a powerful symbol for the company and the regiment, and its loss the worst possible disgrace; for these reasons they were defended with all possible effort, and their capture was the best indication of the seriousness of a defeat.

Weapons

In the early 1600s an infantry company was composed of pikemen, musketeers and calivermen, but English theorists soon followed the Dutch when the latter withdrew the caliver from service in 1609. Companies were then composed only of musketeers and pikemen in approximately equal proportions. This situation did not last, as Sir James Turner commented: 'thereafter the Musket crav'd the half of the Game, and got it, so that each company was equally divided into Pikemen and Musketeers. But equality for the most part is short liv'd, and so far'd it in this, for very soon the Musqueteers challeng'd the two thirds and obtained them, leaving but one third for the pikemen, which for the most part they keep'.

Most English writers in the 1620s and 1630s still held that a company should have equal proportions of pikemen and musketeers, and Trained Band units were still equipped in this way on the eve of the first Bishops' War in 1639; but opinion was beginning to favour an increased ratio of musketeers. (A proportion of pikemen were still necessary, of course, as only the protection they offered could prevent—under most circumstances—an infantry unit being ridden into the ground by a determined and well-timed cavalry

To present well and giue fire, ye musket in the Rest held by ye left hand, the right elbow somewhat vp, & turning the body a little to the left side, the left knee bowed the Right legge straight out, yt it may be held and shot of the surer. Also when he giue fire he shall set ye musket against his brest & then lay his Cheeke to the stocke.

attack.) The contract for Scots infantry agreed in July 1642, for example, specified a ratio of 3:2 (6,000 musketeers to 4,000 pikemen) and this probably represented the state of the art in England. Later in 1642 a ratio of 2:1 became the standard and in October Alderman Andrewes and Stephen Estwick were buying arms for Parliament in France and Holland on this ratio ('twelve thousand muskets and rests, six thousand pikes, six thousand corslets'). This was retained by the New Model Army and was continued throughout the Commonwealth and the armies of Charles II and James II.

This was the theory but the actual availability of weapons often made a nonsense of precise ratios. In the first year of the Civil War Parliamentary regiments were able to draw upon the arsenals of the Tower of London and Hull as well as the private armouries of the City Guilds. This allowed the Parliament to equip infantry in ratios varying between 1:1 and 2:1; but the King's Army was more hard-pressed for equipment, and a ratio of 1:1 would have been more common amongst the Royalists in 1642.

As the war progressed problems of supply were largely overcome, and by 1643 there was probably an effective ratio of 2:1. The position of the Royalist army was complicated by the swift reduction in the relative strength of their regiments as they found it harder to recruit infantry, and the inclusion in their Marching Army of 'Commanded' bodies of musketeers from their garrisons. It is probable that a Royalist regiment would still have been equipped on a 2:1 basis, but the inclusion of detachments of musketeers raised the overall ratio in the Marching Army. This was the experience of regiments in the Marching Armies whose supply was a priority. Garrison units and regiments in the smaller armies were more dependent on local resources and the standard of their equipment varied from the perfect to a burlesque of it.

Two views of the 'Give Fire' posture, showing the butt of the musket held to the right breast, not the shoulder. The first is from an English manual of 1623, and the second from a manual by Henry Hexham printed in 1637. Apart from the helmet, rarely issued to English musketeers, Hexham's illustration provides a good impression of a Civil War musketeer. (British Library, and author's collection)

Give Fire.

Musketeers

At the turn of the century a musketeer 'hath his Sword and Dagger, his Burgenet, his Musket with a rest and Scowring-stick, sometime called a rammer; his flaske turned now into a Bandeler with charges, or Powder-bags; or some fantasticall fellow will carry it in his pocket, trusting to his hand for the Charge; his Touch-box, Powder, Bullet mold, priming Yron, Match, Worm and etc'. Improvements were required as the century progressed as the equipment specified in *Directions for Musters* (1638) indicated. This manual, modelled on the Dutch style, stated: 'The Musketier must be armed with a good Musket, (the Barrel of 4 Foot long, the bore of 12 bullets in the pound rowling in) a rest, Bandelier, Head-piece, a good Sword, Girdle and Hangers'. Although Trained Band musketeers were still expected to wear them, few musketeers still wore helmets on campaign.

Another major change was the introduction of a lighter musket with a shorter barrel, three and a half feet instead of four feet. Muskets of this pattern could be fired without a musket-rest, and from 1643 were issued by both sides without one. This new musket had been recommended by the Board of Ordnance in 1640, but its use during the Civil War depended upon its availability. Old-fashioned and second-hand muskets were imported in large numbers from abroad, particularly Holland, and

these would still require rests. Another problem with these imports was poor quality—as in the case of those received for the king by Captain John Strachan in March 1644, who commented: 'and the musketts, there are about 1000 of them, I am assured they are of 3, or 4 sundry bores, some pistoll

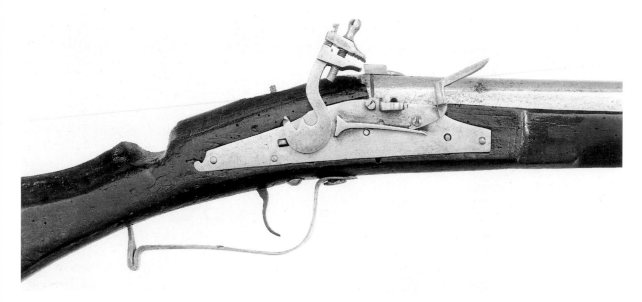

Firelocks. Muskets using types of flintlock rather than smouldering matchcord were commonly used by companies of artillery guards on the basis that they were safer to carry near stocks of gunpowder. A few independent companies of **Royalist infantry were also equipped with them. These are the two most common types, the 'English lock' above, and the 'dog-lock' below. (By courtesy of the Board of Trustees, Royal Armouries)**

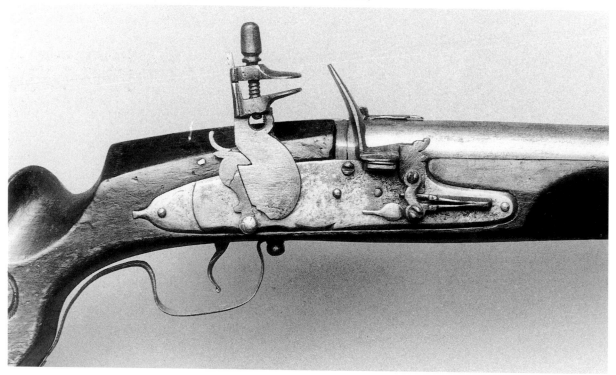

bores, some carbine bores, some little fowling peeces, and all the old trash that could bee rapt together'. Different bores caused considerable supply problems, and some musketeers had to bite pieces off their bullets to make them fit the barrel.

The majority of muskets used during the Civil War were matchlocks such as those described above; but a type of flintlock, termed 'firelocks' by contemporaries, was also in limited use. These were especially popular for companies of artillery guards, since the use of matchlocks, with their lengths of smouldering matchcord had obvious disadvantages when carried near the gunpowder of an artillery train. In addition there were several independent 'Firelock' companies in service in the King's Army.

The matchlock was still a more usefully rugged weapon in action than the 'firelock', since even if the mechanism was broken the musket could be fired by simply 'popping' the match in the priming pan by hand. Its disadvantages were the huge amounts of matchcord required, since even on the march the file-leaders kept theirs alight so that they could light those of the rest of their files if attacked. The consumption of match was also a problem for the garrisons of threatened towns, the garrison of Lyme Regis, for example, 'having in it 1,500 soldiers, including the seamen' who used 'every day and night near $\frac{1}{4}$ tun (five hundredweight) of match'. The city of Stafford overcame this by giving orders for the delivery 'out of the Earle of Denbigh's Magazeene unto the severall Commanders of Foote belonginge to this garrison for every twenty soldiers they have in there severall companies 5 firelock muskets' on the understanding that 'they bringe in the said Firelocks againe which the said Mr. Flower

is to call for when any of the said companies goe to remayne in any other garrison'. This was an intelligent solution for a common problem but was probably exceptional.

Military theorists did see real advantages in the use of the 'firelock' for particular occasions, and Sir James Turner's comments provide a clear impression of the trend: 'It is impossible to hide burning Matches so well in the night-time especially if there be any wind, (though there be covers made of white Iron, like extinguishers purposely for that end) but that some will be seen by a vigilant enemy, and thereby many secret enterprises are lost. It were therefore good, that for the half of the Muskets (if not for them all) flintlocks were made and kept carefully by the Captain of arms of each company, that upon any such occasion or party, the half or more of the other Locks might be immediately taken off, and the flint-ones clapt on by the Gunsmith of the company, and there would be no danger of seeing burning Matches, the sight whereof hath ruin'd many good designs'.

George Monk favoured as an alternative 'that you have in each Company six good Fowling-pieces, of such a length as a soldier may well be able to take aim, and to shoot at ease . . . those souldiers that carry the Fowling-pieces, ought to have command when they come within distance of Shot of that Division of the Enemy that they are to

Matchlock musket. Before firing the musketeer would check that the matchcord in the 'serpent' would touch the centre of the cover which guarded his priming pan. When ready to fire he would swivel the pan cover and pull the trigger to bring the matchcord to the priming powder. This matchlock has a circular depression to mark the check point. (By courtesy of the Board of Trustees, Royal Armouries)

encounter with, that they shoot not at any, but at the Officers of that Division'. There is no evidence that this theory was ever used in battle but there are several instances of marksmen armed with 'fowling-pieces' with rifled barrels picking off gun crews and officers during sieges.

Pikemen

The pike was considered by military authors to be the most honourable weapon and the one fit for a gentleman to carry because, as Richard Elton commented in his *The Compleat Body of the Art Military*, 'it is so in respect of antiquity; for there hath been the use of the Pike and Spear, many hundred years before there was any knowledge of the Musket'. Military theory also held that the 'tallest, biggest, and strongest should be ordered to carry pikes, that they may the better endure the weight of their defensive arms'.

The extent of the pikeman's equipment can be seen from the statutory requirements listed in the manual *Directions for Musters* (1638). This stated: 'the Pikeman must be armed with a Pike seventeen foot long, head and all; (the diameter of the staff to be one inch ¾, the head to be well steeled, 8 inches long, broad, strong, and sword-pointed; the cheeks 2 foot long, well riveted; the butt-end bound with a ring of iron) a Gorget, Back, Breast, Tassets and Head-piece, a good sword of 3 foot long, cutting and stiff-pointed, with Girdle and Hangers'.

The 'cheeks' of the pike were strips of steel riveted to the staff below the head to prevent an opponent hacking it off with a sword. There was some dispute over the optimum length of a pike, as some authorities favoured 15 feet and others, such as George Monk and Sir James Turner, recommended 18 feet. Sixteen feet had become the standard by 1657, when an order for equipment specified they were to be 'made of good ash, 16 feet long, bars to be strong and serviceable, in length to be 2 ft or 22 inches. The staves to be coloured with aquafortis'. Amongst the Trained Bands, whose equipment would have been bought over a period measured in decades, this could result in several different lengths of pike in use together. The same uneven appearance could be found amongst regular soldiers, but for a different reason: Sir James Turner commented, 'In our Modern Wars it is ordr'd by most Princes and States to be eighteen

foot long, yet few exceed fifteen; and if officers be not careful to prevent it, many base soldiers will cut some off the length of that, as I have oft seen it done'. An officer serving in Ireland also commented on this practice, saying rather bitterly: 'Some that were not strong enough in the British Army for his Pike in a windy day would cut off a foot, and some two of their pikes, which is a damned thing to be suffered', an indication that this was a common problem.

The heavy armour was usually carried on carts on the march although it had to be worn if action was imminent. By 1642 it had become the practice to abandon the collar or gorget, and as the war progressed the tassets were dispensed with also. George Monk recommended 'a Buff Girdle of double Buff eight inches broad, the which is to be worn under the Skirts of his Doublet instead of Taces [tassets] . . . I am well assured that a Girdle of

Pikeman's armour: back (left) and breast (right) plates. Note the belt which passes around the waist of the armour to fasten it, and the hole at the base of the backplate. This would have a hook attached from which the pikeman would hang his helmet when on the march. (National Army Museum)

Buff will be much safer, and much more serviceable and easier for a Pike-man to wear than Taces'. Again, this is an experimental idea which may never have been used in practice.

In the years after the Civil War the New Model Army abandoned the use of armour altogether. Sir William Lockhart, commander of the English regiments serving in Flanders, wrote to John Thurloe, Secretary of State, asking 'If his Highness could spare twelve or fifteen hundred corslets for our pikemen, I would accustom them to wear them when they mount guards, and at all other reviews; a

stand of five hundred pikes well armed with headpiece and corslet will be a very terrible thing to be seen in these countries'. By this time most West European infantry had abandoned armour as too much of a restriction for swift marches, the only significant exception being the Dutch.

Dress, Logistics & Management

Uniforms

While uniformed bodies of troops were uncommon in Europe, English soldiers had been issued with uniform coats since Tudor times. The county authorities who were charged with the re-

sponsibility of raising troops for the Crown were obliged to issue them with 'Coat and Conduct' money, i.e. uniform coats, and sufficient funds to pay for their journey, or conducting, to the rendezvous of the Royal army. Different counties favoured different colours, probably according to the local availability of cloth, and white or blue uniform coats were often issued.

The tradition of uniformed units was common, therefore, to both sides at the outbreak of the Civil War, but the choice of colour depended on local supply or the colonel's personal choice. The net result was that units with the same colour coats were commonly found on both sides and the only means of distinction was the 'field sign' or the 'field word' chosen for the day. Examples of field signs are white cloth worn in the hatband or around the arm, and green 'boughs' or sprigs of rosemary. The field word

Uniforms: Coat Colours

Parliament Armies		King's Armies	
Earl of Essex	Tawney Orange	King's Lifeguard	Red
Charles Essex	Tawney Orange	Queen's Lifeguard	Red
Thomas Grantham	Tawney Orange	Prince Rupert's Firelocks	Red
Denzil Holles	Red	Prince Charles	Red
Lord Robartes	Red lined Yellow	Sir Allan Apsley	Red
Lord Peterborough	Red lined Blue	Edward Hopton	Red
Philip Skippon	Red lined Yellow	Prince Rupert	Blue
Anthony Stapley	Red lined Yellow	Ralph Hopton	Blue
Harry Barclay	Red lined Blue	Thomas Lunsford	Blue
John Holmstead	Red lined White	Henry Lunsford	Blue
Randall Mainwaring	Red lined White	Charles Gerard	Blue
Lord Halifax	Red lined Blue	Earl of Northampton	Green
Thomas Rainsborough	Red	Robert Broughton	Green
Edward Montague	Red lined White	Henry Tillier	Green
Sir Thomas Fairfax	Red lined Blue	Thomas Pinchbeck	Grey
Lord Brooke	Purple	Sir Henry Bard	Grey
Lord Rochford	Blue lined White	Sir Ralph Dutton	White
Earl of Stamford	Blue	Sir Stephen Hawkins	White
Sir Henry Cholmley	Blue	Marquis of Newcastle	White
Sir William Constable	Blue	Lord Percy	White
Lord Saye & Sele	Blue	Sir Thomas Blackwell	Black
Lord Mandeville	Blue	Sir Gilbert Talbot	Yellow
George Langham	Blue lined White	Sir Matthew Appleyard	Yellow
Sir Arthur Haselrige	Blue	Sir John Paulet	Yellow
George Payne	Blue	Sir Charles Vavasour	Yellow
John Hampden	Green lined Yellow		
Samuel Jones	Green		
Earl of Manchester	Green lined Red		
Sir John Merrick	Grey		
Thomas Ballard	Grey lined White		
Sir John Gell	Grey		
Simon Rugeley	Grey		
Richard Browne	Grey		
Sir William Brook	White		

The Deliverance of St Peter (Acts xii, 6-10) by David Teniers the Younger; in accordance with contemporary practice, the 'Roman' guards wear 17th century costume. A good view of soldiers' costume; note the sergeant's sash and gold-embroidered buff coat, and the gorget in the bottom left. (Wallace Collection)

or battle cry was usually something simple such as 'God and the Cause' or 'For God and Parliament'. This reduced the confusion somewhat; but on occasion both sides adopted identical field signs and on at least one occasion the same battle cry. Several officers were captured through wrongly assuming the soldiers they rode up to were on the same side.

When first raised regiments were uniformed in a wide variety of colours including red, blue, green, yellow, white or grey, black and even purple. A chart showing some of the known examples is included here. To some extent regional supplies of cloth created a semblance of uniformity in the armies; e.g. the Marquis of Newcastle's famous 'whitecoats' and the issue of clothing to the King's Oxford Army 'some all in red, coates, breeches and mounteers; & some all in blewe' in 1643. The most significant development of all, however, was the issue of uniforms to the New Model Army, where, 'the men are redcoats all, the whole army only are distinguished by several facings of their coats'. This colour was continued throughout the Protectorate

and was retained at the Restoration in the new Royal Army to become the national colour. The 'facings' were probably the linings of the soldiers' coats which showed where the cuffs were turned back, and may have matched the tape strings used to fasten the coats.

The question of the clothing actually issued is less certain, and it is possible some county soldiers were distinguished only by ribbons in their hats. An impression of the basic aim can be seen from the order of September 1642 for clothing English soldiers in Ulster. This specified a cap, canvas doublet, cassock, breeches, two pairs of stockings, two pairs of shoes and two shirts for each soldier. The troops in Parliament's new army did not fare quite so well, but orders were given for the issue of 'coats, shoes, shirts and caps' to each soldier in

25

August 1642. There is no record of the caps actually being issued, but one other item—the soldier's snapsack—was. This was an early form of soldier's pack in which he carried any spare clothing, food or plunder he had acquired. The same equipment—coats, shoes, shirts and snapsacks—were issued to Essex's infantry in 1643; and not until its re-equipping after the Lostwithiel disaster in 1644 were breeches and caps issued to his army. The terms 'cassocks' and 'coats' seem to have been interchangeable. The equipment of local troops is less certain, and must have varied greatly with local conditions.

The issue of clothing to the King's Army is not so well documented, but the Royalist entrepreneur Thomas Bushell undertook to provide 'souldiers Cassocks, Breeches, Stockings and Capps' for the king's forces in March 1642, and those of his infantry in Oxford in 1643 certainly received matching suits of coats, breeches and Montero caps.

A tavern scene by David Teniers the Younger. This gives a useful view of the shirt and breeches often concealed by the soldier's coat in contemporary illustrations. (Wallace Collection)

The breeches and caps represented an improvement on the issue to Parliament soldiers, who had to wear their own, and there is no reason to suppose Royalist units were any worse clothed than their opponents. This was not altogether encouraging, however, as the quality of clothing was often poor, and after a few weeks' campaigning it was often reduced almost to rags.

Officers and non-commissioned officers wore their own civilian clothes, with the exception of the corporals (and lanspassadoes, if any) who wore regimental uniform, and drummers, who wore whatever their colonel or captain chose. The only exception to this is provided by officers serving in Ireland, who were issued with more expensive clothing, the cost of which was to be deducted from their pay.

Pay

Pay was a critical factor in the success or failure of armies as without 'constant' or regular pay there could be no discipline, and without discipline it was not possible to achieve the standards of military training necessary for victory. An equally important consequence of regular pay was the warmth or otherwise of popular opinion: unpaid soldiers were obliged to live at 'free quarter', that is they lived at the expense of the local people in whose homes they were billeted but paid nothing. This could easily become a vicious and detestable habit. Both sides resorted to the 'free quarter' on occasion, but where the Parliament at least made efforts to restrict it, King Charles allowed his commanders a great deal more licence. As Clarendon commented, 'the country was both to feed and clothe the soldier, which quickly inclined them to remember only the burden and forget the quarrel'.

The level of pay varied slightly in different areas but was based on the standard used in England before the Civil War. (The daily rates quoted are, of course, in the pre-decimal system where 12 pence make a shilling and 20 shillings a pound.) The colonel, lieutenant-colonel and sergeant major drew pay and allowances both as staff officers and as captains of their own companies.

In addition to their pay officers had an allowance for wagons to transport their possessions at the rate of two for the colonel, one each for the lieutenant-colonel and sergeant major, and one between two for the captains. Their higher rates of pay and allowances made the officers' position quite comfortable even if they did not receive all of it. The position of the common soldier was rather worse, as deductions were made at source for his food and uniform, leaving perhaps a shilling a week owed in cash. The deductions were resented all the more because unscrupulous army contractors commonly sold poor-quality clothing at twice its real value. This was bad enough, but another valid complaint was that deductions were still made regardless of whether clothing or food had ever been issued.

From the very beginning of the War both sides found it impossible to pay their men in full, and in 1644 the Parliament was reduced to the expedient of putting all officers above the rank of captain on half-pay for the duration. The Ordinance for the New Model Army caught the captains as well, and stated 'every Captain both of Horse and Foot, and every other Inferior and Superior Officer, or other, in the said Army, whose Pay comes to Ten Shillings a day, or above, shall take but half the pay due to him and shall respite the other half upon the Publick Faith'. When three months' pay was due a certificate was issued to the officer.

The pay of the Royalist forces was certainly based on the same model, but its frequency and the level of

Staff	Pounds	Per Day Shillings	Pence
Colonel	1	4	0
Lieutenant-Colonel		12	0
Sergeant-Major		8	0
Preacher		4	0
Provost		4	0
Chirurgeon		4	0
Quartermaster		4	0
Wagon-master		3	0
Chirurgeon's Mate		2	0
Drum Major		1	4

Company	Pounds	Per Day Shillings	Pence
Captain		12	0
Lieutenant		4	0
Ensign		3	0
Sergeant		1	4
Corporal		1	0
Gentleman at Arms		1	0
Drummer		1	0
Clerk		1	0
Lanspassadoe		0	10
Soldier		0	8

deductions are less certain. Royalist administration was certainly more wasteful of resources than the Parliament's, but there is evidence that it was able to obtain considerable sums, and the king's soldiers were probably no worse paid than the Parliament's. One problem was, of course, that for the common soldier this was not very much, and Royal officers seem to have been more ready to allow plunder and pillage to keep their men contented.

Discipline

A comparison is often made between the 'riotous' king's armies and the 'godly' Parliament soldiers. There is some truth in this, especially if comparisons are made between the New Model Army and General Goring's army in the West in 1646; but both sides had suffered from indiscipline at the outset. When first raised, Parliament soldiers had plundered the homes of Catholics and other 'Malignants' in the London suburbs; and the letters of Sergeant Nehemiah Wharton show that they continued the practice as they marched through the counties. They were equally likely to seize plunder from one another, as an extract from one of Wharton's letters shows: 'A troop of horse belonging to Colonel Foynes met me, and pillaged me of all, and robbed me of my very sword for which cause I told them I would rather have my sword or dye in the field, commaunded my men to charge with bullet [i.e. load their muskets], and by devisions to fire upon them, which made them with shame return my sword'. He had his revenge when on guard at Northampton, when he stopped the same troop on its way out of the town and 'searched every horseman of that troop to the skin, took from them a fat buck, a venison pasty ready baked, but lost my own goods'.

Royalist soldiers were as unruly, as recorded by the cavalryman Captain Richard Atkins who recalled on one occasion: 'Observing a hole in an elder hedge, I put in my hand and pulled out a bag of money; which if our foot had espied (who were also upon the search) they had certainly taken me for an enemy, and deprived me of both life and it'.

Apart from the problems of plundering, in-discipline hindered training in the use of arms and battle tactics. A comment by Wharton in August 1642 shows how serious a problem this was: 'This evening our ungodly Lieutenant Colonel, upon an ungrounded whimsey, commaunded two of our Captains, namely, Captain Francis and Captain Beacon, with their companies, to march out of the towne but they went not'. Six Parliament colonels wrote formally to the Earl of Essex in September, insisting that he take firm measures as 'the truth is unless we were able to execute some exemplary punishment upon the principal malefactors, we have no hope to redress this horrid enormity. We beseech your Excellency to take this into your present and serious consideration, for if this go on awhile the army will grow as odious to the Country as the Cavaliers'.

The solution for both sides was the enforcement of Articles of War, a list of offences and the punishments due based on the codes used before the war. Just to cover all eventualities, the last clause contained a catch-all such as 'All other Faults, Disorders, and Offences not mentioned in these Articles shall be punished according to the general customs and Laws of War'. It had always been customary for army commanders to issue these standing orders, and the king and the Earl of Essex both published essentially similar versions in 1642. Their success as a deterrent depended, of course, on the degree to which they were enforced.

While there are instances of examples being made of soldiers on both sides, these men were clearly unlucky rather than typical. Only with regular pay, or something approaching it, was a commander able to enforce discipline successfully. The king's armies were never able to achieve this, possibly because of the poor example set by the king himself: King Charles had a very casual attitude to the enforcement of the articles, and allowed his officers considerable licence, particularly when dealing with those he considered disloyal. This was aggravated by the influence of those of his officers with professional experience, who introduced the harsh attitude to civilians which they had learnt in the vicious wars in Europe or Ireland. The alienation of the civilian population which this attitude fostered was to prove a serious, perhaps a crucial, factor in the king's defeat.

Sir Thomas Fairfax made the most of the fresh opportunity offered by the formation of a better-paid New Model Army 'to lay an early foundation of good success in the punishment of former disorders and the prevention of future misdemeanours', by holding a court martial and marching the Army past the tree on which he hung two offenders. With this attitude, and the cash payment he was able to offer for provisions he made, the New Model Army appear a distinct improvement over the type of soldiers most contemporaries were used to. Fairfax's more strictly disciplined men did not prove better fighting infantrymen than the King's when they met at Naseby; but their more controlled behaviour won them local support. This became crucially important, as Fairfax's first campaign coincided with the outbreak of the Clubman Associations in some 15 counties in England and Wales. While not all the Clubmen groups were prepared to support Fairfax by fighting for him, they were universally distrustful of the king's promises, and denied the Royalist cause urgently needed funds and recruits.

Victuals

Sir James Turner's comment on the provisions for soldiers is based on his experience in Europe, but does give a good impression of a complete system, while references during the Civil War give individual examples. Turner's description was: 'There are few princes who have not their particular establishment for their proviant, both in field and garrison, as well as for money; the order whereof commonly is this: they allow so much bread, flesh, wine or beer to every trooper and foot soldier, which ordinarily is alike to both, then they allow to the officers, according to their dignities and charges, double, triple and quadruple portions; as to an Ensign four times more than to a common soldier, a Colonel commonly having twelve portions allowed him. The ordinary allowance for a soldier in the field is daily, two pound of bread, one pound of flesh, or in lieu of it, one pound of cheese, one pottle of wine, or in lieu of it, two pottles of beer. It is enough cry the soldiers, we desire no more, it is enough in conscience. But this allowance will not last very long, they must be contented to march sometimes one whole week, and scarce get two pounds of bread all the while, and their officers as well as they'. The English evidently used a similar system, as the rations specified for English soldiers in Ireland in 1642 was set at one pound of bread, one pound of beef or a half-pound of cheese or fish in lieu, and a quarter-pound of butter.

For the most part armies on the march were quartered in the towns and villages along their route. The householder was then obliged to provide food and lodging in return for a certificate, redeemable by the army paymaster. In this case the supplies would be on the basis described above but would depend on the householder's larder. Where supplies were carried with the army itself the victual was usually bread, biscuit, peas, butter, Cheshire cheese, bacon and beer. Sometimes a small herd of cattle or sheep accompanied the army to provide fresh meat.

In garrison or where an army remained static as besiegers, a system of requisitions was used. Warrants were issued to the local county authorities for provisions to be brought in. Examples of this type of provisions include beef, bacon, pork, salt herrings, mutton, wheat, oats, beans, peas and beer. Most garrisons, even if besieged, kept live sheep and cattle, the latter for dairy produce as well as meat. Fresh food was considered important, as in the opinion of the Earl of Cork salt beef, barrelled biscuits and butter, with water to drink made only for 'a rich churchyard and a weak garrison'.

Mutiny

The most famous mutinies of the Civil War were those of the New Model Army in 1647; but these must be seen in their context and mutiny was, in fact, a constant part of military life in the first half of the 17th century.

Organised mutiny was developed to a fine art in the 16th century among the soldiers of the Spanish Army of Flanders, whose pay was constantly in arrears. Some incident, perhaps trivial, ignited smouldering discontent; and the soldiers of a garrison, regiment or a whole army would band together to demand their pay and improvements in their conditions, such as a hospital, and payments to the sick and the legatees of the dead. The mutineers then elected a leader and a council to advise him, and negotiated with their commander. The effect of increasingly frequent mutinies on the Spanish campaigns in the Low Countries can be imagined; but it was the only effective form of seeking redress available to the common soldier, and was soon adopted in other European armies. Even the Swedish Army mutinied over arrears of pay in 1633 and again in 1635; and smaller mutinies occurred among troops in the well-paid Dutch service.

Professional soldiers with experience gained in the Thirty Years War introduced the idea of collective bargaining to English and Scottish armies. A notable example was the mutiny of the Scottish army hired, but irregularly paid, by the English Parliament to suppress the popular revolt in Ireland. By the autumn of 1642 discontent had arisen and the officers, 'finding themselves ill payd, and which was worse, not knowing in the time of the civill warr [i.e. in England] who should be their paymaster, and reflecting on the successful issue of the National Covenant of Scotland, bethought themselves of making one also; but they were wise enough to give it ane other name, and therefore christened it a "Mutual Assurance" '. The Earl of Leven, who had only recently arrived to take command of the Army, failed to crush this 'Mutual Assurance' and returned to Scotland. The officers then formed a permanent council of officers with their commander, Robert Monro, as president. This council had a strong say in the conduct and activities of the army thereafter.

In England mutinies of small garrisons were commonplace, whether over the removal of an unpopular commander such as Colonel John Venn, Governor of Windsor; or more commonly as Captain Denys Taylor's report on the mutiny at Henley shows, 'the occasion of the mutiny was that no more money came down'. The circumstances of the Civil War itself also weakened authority as it was not a long step from questioning the authority of the king to disputing that of officers. As Lieutenant-Colonel Mark Gryme commented after one mutiny: 'All that I can do is little enough to appease them seeing their pay is so little, and private incendiaries many'.

The mutinies of the New Model Army must be seen against a background in which soldiers or officers would naturally see mutiny as a means to secure what was due to them. In the New Model Army the chief grievances were their considerable arrears of pay (18 weeks for the Foot and 43 weeks for the Horse and Dragoons) and their need for an indemnity for acts committed during the war. The indemnity was crucially important, for, as a surgeon in the Northern Army warned his fellows, 'If they had not an act of indemnity they should be most of them hanged when they were reduced [i.e. disbanded]: and for an example, told them the judges had hanged fourteen soldiers already which took horses by order from their officers'.

Neither the mutiny itself nor the formation of 'Conventions of Officers' and the election of agents or 'Agitators' by the private soldiers, first in the Horse and then the Foot, are outside contemporary military practice. The politicisation of the Army and its connection with the Levelling movement were certainly radical departures, but this developed after the mutiny had already brought the Army into conflict with the Parliament.

Training

The first stage in the training of any soldier was, as the Drillmaster William Barriffe said, 'the well-managing and handling of their Armes: which may easily be attained by frequent Practice, and the Souldiers thereby brought to use them with ease, safety, and delight: where on the contrary (without

The Front before closing

exercise) the easiest Armes become not only troublesome burthens unto the unskilful bearers, but too often prove dangerous and hurtfull, both to themselves and fellowes, that rank and file with them'. It was the responsibility of the corporals of the company, under the overall supervision of the sergeants, to train their men how to use pike or musket according to a set series of 'postures' or movements. The large number of training postures were only used as an aid to training and were reduced in action, those for musketeers being reduced to three: 'Make Ready; Present; Give Fire'.

Once they were proficient enough to be reasonably safe in a group, soldiers were formed into the files they would fight in. The file was the basic sub-unit of the company and was 'a sequence of men, standing one behind another, back to belly, in a straight line from Front to Reere, consisting sometimes of six, eight or ten men, on some occasions the Spaniards make them twelve deep'. In 1642 the French and Swedish used files of six men, the English used eight and the Dutch still kept to ten. The files were then drawn into groups either of musketeers or of pikemen for training by the sergeants in the five basic aspects of the drill: Distances, Facings, Doublings, Countermarches and Wheelings. These groups would form the next sub-unit of the company, which was sometimes called a 'squadron' in the Dutch and English service, or a 'corporallship' in the Swedish.

The next stage was to draw all the squadrons of the company together for tactical training under the supervision of the captain and his lieutenant. The drill manuals of the day showed a formidable

Infantry drill from John Bingham's *Tactiks of Aelian* (1616). This series of three illustrations shows the sequence used to bring files closer together. The left-hand file remains stationary while the others turn to face it, close the distance and then face front.

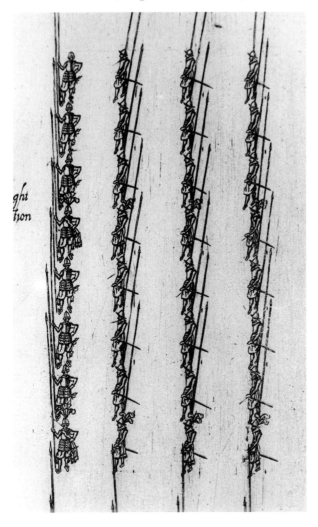

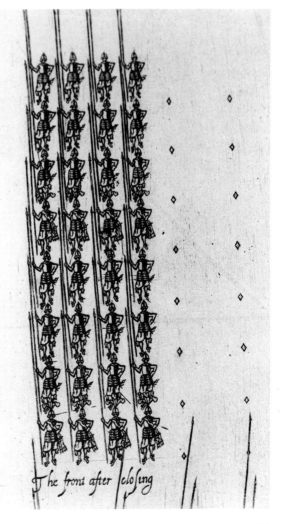

31

number of different tactical styles, but as William Barriffe comments, a captain should 'make use of so many of them, as he shall think fit for his present occasion or exercise'. It is this choice of the essential forms of drill which the Earl of Essex referred to in the opening months of the Civil War when he instructed his officers not to attempt too much with the newly raised soldiers, but 'to bring them to use their arms readily and expertly, and not to busy them in practising the ceremonious forms of military discipline'.

The manuals show a series of tactical formations for the company, but these are simply a training aid, as the company itself was not used as a tactical formation in the field. In action the tactical formation was the regiment, which was divided into three or four 'Grand Divisions' each composed of two or three of the regiment's companies. Each Grand Division was formed in the tactical style taught in company training: a centre of pikemen with wings of musketeers on each flank. To achieve this the regiment's sergeant major drew up its companies and divided them among the Grand

Divisions; he would then draw out the pikemen from the companies which were to form each separate Grand Division to combine them to form its centre, and then divided the musketeers in two bodies, one for each flank.

Although the King's Army at Edgehill was drawn up in the complex Swedish tactical style this was unusual, and the English usually preferred the simpler Dutch style for their newly raised soldiers. To judge from Richard Elton's work, *The Compleat Body of the Art Military*, printed after the Civil War, the experience of five years of campaigning did finally produce officers and soldiers capable of successfully performing the more complex styles.

Into Battle

The basic training described above was sufficient to allow a commander to form up his regiments of foot in the open. This was usually in two lines, with the units positioned so that those in the second line covered the gaps between those in the first, rather like the pieces on a draughts board. Battles such as Edgehill or Naseby were fought on sites which allowed this classic style to be used.

A commander with a weaker force, or simply a better eye for the advantages of the ground, might

An enlarged view of the New Model infantry at Naseby, from Joshua Sprigge's *Anglia Rediviva* (1647). Note the 'Forlorn Hope' of musketeers, the artillery pieces sited between regiments, and Lt.-Col. Pride's Regiment in second line. (D. Carter collection)

Peace: The Artillery Garden, c. 1620
1: The Double-Armed Man
2: Pikeman
3: Musketeer

1   2   3   A

Recruitment: Oxford, 1643
1: Company Clerk
2: Officer, King's Lifeguard of Foot
3: Drummer, King's Lifeguard of Foot

B

Plunder: The Earl of Essex's Army, 1642
1: Musketeer, John Hampden's Regiment
2: Musketeer, Thomas Ballard's Regiment
3: Pikeman, Lord Robartes' Regiment

2

1

3

C

Training: Royalist musketeers
1: Musketeer, Royal Army, 1642
2: Musketeer, King's Oxford Army, 1643
3: 'Firelock', Capt. Sanford's Firelocks, 1643

D

Tavern: Col. Samuel Jones's Regiment, 1643   1: Fifer   2: Musketeer   3: Pikeman

E

Skirmish: The Westminster Trained
Bands, Basing House, 1643
1: Officer
2: Ensign
3, 4, 5, 6: Musketeers

Angus McBride

3   2   1   F

Encampment: Army of the
Solemn League & Covenant, 1644
1: Sergeant
2: Musketeer
3: Musketeer
4: Minister

G

Battle: New Model Army, Naseby, 1645
1, 2: Pikeman & musketeer, Sir Thomas Fairfax's Regiment
3: Ensign, Prince Rupert's Regiment

3   1   2

H

Aftermath: Marston Moor, 1644
1: Pikeman, Marquis of Newcastle's Regiment
2: Musketeer, Earl of Manchester's Regiment
3: Surgeon

I

Musketeers' equipment
1: Musketeers
2: Hats & Montero caps
3, 4: Bandoleers & tools
5: Muskets

J

Pikeman's equipment

2: Helmets & Monmouth caps

1: Pikemen

1

2

2

4

1

5

3

3

3: Armour & pikeheads
4, 5: Rapiers, backswords etc.

Angus McBride

K

choose more broken country, especially if he had fewer cavalry than his opponents. Sir William Waller, in particular, was famous for this, as the Royalist Lieutenant-Colonel Walter Slingsby's comment shows: 'Indeed that Generall of the Rebells was the best shifter and chooser of the ground when he was not master of the field that I ever saw, which are great abilityes in a Souldier'.

In broken or wooded country the personal fighting qualities of the soldier and his ability to use his weapons were more important than the unit drill he had been taught. For this kind of scrambling action over ditches and hedgerows, files of musketeers were drawn out from their regiments and formed into separate 'commanded' bodies, as pikemen were of little use. Contemporary commanders held the view that brave but poorly trained soldiers could be used in the open but would stand little chance against veterans in this 'hedge-fighting'. In 1648, for example, when the Scots army invaded England at the opening of the Second Civil War, Sir James Turner favoured the route through Yorkshire rather than Lancashire 'and for this reason only, that I understood Lancashire was a close country, full of ditches and hedges, which was a great advantage the English would have over our raw and undisciplined musketeers, the Parliament's army consisting of experienced and well trained sojors and excellent firemen; on the other hand Yorkshire being a more open countrey and full of heaths, where we both might make use of our horse, and come sooner to push of pike'.

The clash of major armies was only a part of the war; all over the country smaller forces contended for control of territory or strongpoints such as fortified towns or country houses, or simply conducted plundering raids. Swift marching and sudden surprise was the key to success in these small actions. To achieve this both sides commonly formed forces composed of cavalry, dragoons and 'commanded' musketeers, often providing horses for the musketeers or having them ride double with the cavalry troopers. Sir William Waller, whose liking for swift night marches earned him the name 'Night Owl', took this a stage further, and made serious but unsuccessful efforts in 1644 to mount all his infantry with the intention of using the mobility this offered to make up for inferior numbers.

The Effigie of the most magnanimous & christ-pursuit GEORGE Duke of Albemarle Earle of Torrington, Baron MONCK of Potheridge, Beauchamp, and Teyes

George Monk, a professional soldier who served in Europe and in the Royal Army in Ireland. He was placed in the Tower of London after his capture at the Battle of Nantwich, but later served Oliver Cromwell. Monk enjoyed the close support of the army he commanded in Scotland, and his influence was the key factor in the Restoration of Charles II.

A Last Word.

George Monk had the last word in the Civil Wars since it was his support which made possible the Restoration of Charles II. It seems proper, therefore, to end with his advice: 'It is most necessary for a General in the first place to approve his Cause, and settle an opinion of right in the minds of his Officers and Souldiers: the which can be no way better done, than by the Chaplains of his Army. Also a General ought to speak to the Colonels of his Army to encourage their Officers with a desire to fight with the Enemy; and all the Officers to do the like to their Souldiers. And the better to raise the common Souldiers spirits, let their Officers tell them that their General doth promise them, if they will fight courageously with their Enemy, and do get the day that they shall have, besides the Pillage of the Field, twelve-pence apiece to drink, to refresh their spirits when the business is done. The which I am confident will make the common men fight better, than the best Oration in the world'.

Further Reading.

There are a whole host of books on the Civil War and its military, political and social aspects. Listed below are some of the most useful military works.

Bariffe, A Civil War Drill Book (Partizan Press, 1988)

C.H. Firth, *Cromwell's Army* (London, 1905, 1921 and 1962)

R. Hutton, *The Royalist War Effort 1642–1646* (Longman, 1982)

J. Kenyon, *The Civil Wars of England* (Weidenfeld & Nicolson, 1988)

J.L. Malcolm, *Caesar's Due: Loyalty and King Charles 1642–1646* (Royal Historical Society, 1983)

S. Peachey & A. Turton, *Old Robin's Foot: the equipping and campaigns of Essex's Infantry 1642–1645* (Partizan Press, 1987)

K.A.B. Roberts, *London & Liberty: Ensigns of the London Trained Bands* (Partizan Press, 1987)

I. Ryder, *An English Army for Ireland* (Partizan Press, 1987)

D. Stevenson, *Scottish Covenanters and Irish Confederates* (Ulster Historical Foundation, 1981)

P. Young and R. Holmes, *The English Civil War, A Military History of the Three Civil Wars 1642–1651* (London, 1974)

A very useful forum for those with an interest in the latest developments of this period is the magazine *English Civil War Notes and Queries* published by Partizan Press at 26 Cliffsea Grove, Leigh-on Sea, Essex SS9 1NQ.

Three views of the position 'Order Your Pike'. The first is a close copy from Jacob de Gheyn's *Exercise of Arms* (1607), the second from an English manual of 1623, and the third a statuette c.1638 from Cromwell House in Highgate. Note how closely de Gheyn's original design was followed. The statuette gives a good impression of the appearance of a pikeman during the Civil War. (Author's collection, British Library and by courtesy of the Board of Trustees, Royal Armouries)

The Plates

A: Peace—The Artillery Garden, c.1620

This plate shows members of the Society of the Artillery Garden practising with their arms in the 'Artillery Garden' from which the name derived. The society was a voluntary association of some of the wealthier London citizens who gathered together to practise weapon-handling and drill, often under the tuition of professional soldiers. Although sometimes mocked by outsiders, the Society did provide a good grounding in these military arts, and its form of training prepared members for their traditional roles as officers of the Militia regiments of the City of London. Members of the Society took their exercises seriously, although as much with the intention of excelling in a social accomplishment as with any intention of military preparation. There was no formal uniform for the Society at this time, and members wore their equipment over their civilian clothing. Their equipment conformed to statutory requirements but was often chosen more with an eye to display than the latest developments. Illustrations dating from 1642 show members carrying old-fashioned heavy muskets rather than the lighter pattern then being produced.

A1: The Double-Armed Man

The English still felt a patriotic nostalgia for the longbow, and its general replacement with firearms had been achieved with some reluctance during Queen Elizabeth's reign. William Neade hoped to re-introduce the national weapon by his invention of a device which allowed a pikeman to attach a longbow to the centre of his pike, so enabling him to hold both in left hand while drawing the bow with his right. It remained popular amongst the voluntary associations in London, particularly for displays, and theorists such as Sir Thomas Kellie and William Barriffe recommended it. There is no evidence that it was ever practised in the field. This citizen is practising Neade's style and so wears the full equipment of a pikeman—gorget, back and breast, tassets, sword and helmet—in addition to the quiver and wristguard of an archer. The trim of leather strips to the shoulders of the armour and the red plume in his helmet are a conscious imitation of the supposed military dress of the Classical past while his boots show the world that here is a man of substance who normally rides—or at least could, if he chose.

Order your Pike.

I

How ye Soldier standing still shall hold the Pike iust before his right foot, gouerning it against ye thumbe, his arme a little bended, & his hand about ye height of his eyes, being not bound alwaies to set the right foot forward.

A2: Pikeman

This citizen wears the full equipment of a pikeman as specified by statute, and stands in the classic 'Order Your Pike' position from the drill manual. Neither this man nor his double-armed colleague have water-proofed their armour by blackening or russeting it, preferring instead the display of polished metal. As these amateur enthusiasts were wealthy men, often fabulously so, they would not be polishing it themselves.

A3: Musketeer

The musketeer has laid down his equipment—musket, musket-rest and matchcord—on the ground beside him in the manner prescribed in the manuals. He retains his bandoleer, the heavy cross-hilted sword hung from his baldric, and wears the helmet which completes his statutory equipment. Note the expensive musket stock, elaborately inlaid with ivory, and the gold-trimmed sleeveless buff-coat.

Two views of the 'Saluting Posture' of a musketeer, one from a manual of 1623 and the other a statuette from Cromwell House, Highgate. Again, the posture is copied from de Gheyn's original design. The statuette dates from c.1638, but gives a good impression of a musketeer of the Civil War. (By courtesy of the Boards of Trustees of the British Library and the Royal Armouries)

Hold in y*e* musket with y*e* Rest, y*e* left hand onely in ballance

38

So standing the Musket in the Rest ballanced, he may gouerne y*e* same with y*e* left hand only and so free y*e* right hand as this figure sheweth.

B: Recruitment; Oxford, 1643

In the early years of the war men volunteered for service under King or Parliament either through a sense of commitment to the cause or for the wages offered (but seldom paid in full) by recruiting officers. By 1644 most of the infantry of either side were raised by impressment. This plate shows a typical scene in Oxford in 1643, with an officer accompanied by a drummer and a clerk recruiting soldiers for the King's Lifeguard.

B1: Company Clerk

The Company clerk records the name of a new recruit in the company's muster roll. This officer kept the company's records of soldiers present and payments received. Contemporary writers specified that he ought to be 'very just and honest', a sure indication that many were not. As an officer he wears his own civilian clothing with the addition of the sword a man of his status would only have worn in military service.

B2: Officer, King's Lifeguard of Foot

With the exception of the corporals, who wore the regimental coat, and the drummers, who wore whatever the colonel or their captain chose, officers on both sides wore their own civilian clothing. The only indications of rank being a sash and the weapons carried—a partizan for a commissioned officer or a halberd for a sergeant. The usual practice was to wear a sash in the 'General's colours' and this officer wears the red sash of his king's service, a feature commonly seen in William Dobson's portraits of gentlemen in the King's Oxford Army. The only other item of military equipment he wears is the gorget at his throat, as his rapier is a part of any gentleman's civilian costume.

B3: Drummer, King's Lifeguard of Foot

Each company of infantry had two drummers on the strength, and each was expected to know 'how to beat all the several points of War' as the drum was used to convey orders in battle or on the march. A drummer was expected to be a mature, intelligent man, the use of drummer boys belonging to a later century as the drum itself was heavy and one of his duties was to carry messages to the enemy and perform the duties of a spy in the process. The drummer's costume was at the discretion of his commander and that of this figure is based upon an

Frontispiece of a satirical pamphlet printed shortly after the Battle of Edgehill. Its text is a pornographic parody of the usual instructions for the drill postures—the first pornographic drill book. . . The antiquated dress of the Welshmen illustrated is part of the satire, and it would be wrong to assume Welsh infantry actually looked like this. (British Library)

illustration of a drummer of the Gardes Françaises, c.1632. The coat colour, red, was that of the Lifeguard at this time, and the design on the drum itself is taken from the well-known portrait of Sir Edmund Walker, the King's Secretary at War. Note particularly the size of the drum and the 'underarm' method of beating it

C: Plunder: The Earl of Essex's Army 1642

Many soldiers on both sides took the opportunities offered by the disruption of Civil War to intimidate and plunder civilians. For the bored soldiers of the Earl of Essex's Army this was a popular pastime in the suburbs of London, and later in the counties as they marched on campaign. They had no authority to do anything more than search for arms, and even then only under the authority of an officer. In fact, as contemporary records show, soldiers plundered at will, showing pretended papers of authority if challenged. When queried by the local sheriff on one occasion they simply refused to let him read the papers, and when he seized their stolen property they returned in greater numbers to recover it and then sold it in the streets. Here an elderly Catholic sits in despair as his home is stripped bare.

C1: Musketeer, Hampden's Regiment

The Ringleader waves a paper claiming it gives him authority for his activity. On enlistment in 1642 Parliament soldiers were supposed to be issued with coats, shoes, shirts, snapsacks and caps. It is not clear whether the use of the word 'caps' at this time

meant anything more precise than headgear, and there is some doubt whether those mentioned in Parliament's orders of 6th August 1642 were ever actually issued. Three styles of headgear are known to have been worn: a Montero cap, a broad-brimmed felt hat, or a Monmouth cap. Breeches were not a general issue for soldiers in the Parliament army until their re-clothing after the debacle at Lostwithiel in 1644, and each continued to wear those he had when he enlisted, or replaced them by theft when possible. This man wears the green uniform coat of his regiment, with its yellow lining showing where the cuffs are turned back, and a Montero cap. He carries his cheap cross-hilted sword on a baldric, and wears the bandoleer which contains powder and shot for the musket he has left in camp. The matchcord he uses to fire his musket is looped over the bandoleer.

C2: Musketeer, Thomas Ballard's Regiment

This man wears a broad-brimmed felt hat with a political pamphlet thrust behind the hatband, and the grey coat of his regiment. His equipment is similar to that of C1, but note the more modern pattern of sword and the different style of bandoleer. Parliament obtained equipment for

A statuette from Cromwell House of a Trained Band drummer c.1638; and a surviving example of a 17th century drum. (By courtesy of the Board of Trustees, Royal Armouries)

their new regiments from a number of different sources: the arsenal at the Tower of London, the military stores of the 'Irish Adventurers' (private subscribers for forces to suppress the Irish revolt), the armouries of the London Guilds, and purchase from abroad. A variety of different styles of equipment could be seen in use by the same regiment.

C3: Pikeman, Lord Robartes' Regiment

The simple set of armour he wears over his red regimental coat has been blackened, a common precaution against rust. He wears a knitted 'Monmouth' cap, a popular style for pikemen as it provided useful padding for the helmet worn in action.

D: Training: Royalist Musketeers

The three musketeers are each equipped in a different style. The first carries a heavy-pattern musket with the musket-rest it requires, and a bandoleer. The second has a lighter musket and has discarded his musket-rest; he carries his ammunition in a 'Powder-Bag' on his waist belt. The third carries a 'dog-lock' musket with the usual bandoleer. Regardless of the type of equipment, continuous training was required to achieve proficiency with a musket.

D1: Musketeer, Royal Army, 1642

This volunteer still wears the clothes he enlisted in, with a red hatband to show his allegiance to his king. His heavy musket is an old-fashioned model, one of many seized by the king as the county Trained Bands were disarmed to provide weapons for the King's Army. Even so, this man is fortunate to have a complete set of equipment, as Clarendon's comments on the state of the army show: 'By all those means together, the Foot, all but three or four hundred, who marched without any weapon but a Cudgel, were Arm'd with Muskets, and Bags for their Powder, and Pikes; but in the whole Body, there was not a Pikeman had a Corslet, and very few Musqueteers who had Swords'. This is an exaggeration as there would certainly have been a substantial number of sets of pikemen's armour in the Trained Band arsenals, but the King's Army was certainly very poorly equipped when it was first raised.

A statuette from Cromwell House of a Trained Band fifer c.1638. Fifers do not appear in contemporary pay records but other references show they were in service, possibly paid for by their colonels personally. (By courtesy of the Board of Trustees, Royal Armouries)

D2: Musketeer, King's Oxford Army, 1643

This soldier wears a 'Powder-Bag' containing paper cartridges with a flask containing priming powder suspended beneath it. These were issued as a temporary expedient to overcome a shortage of bandoleers. An order for the delivery of stores for the manufacture of these powder-bags shows that they were made of 'Calfe skinns tanned and oyled'. His uniform coat, breeches and montero cap are part of the issue of 1643 provided by the entrepreneur Thomas Bushell who reclothed the Oxford infantry in suits of all-red or all-blue.

D3: 'Firelock' Captain Sanford's Firelocks, 1643

With the agreement of a truce in Ireland, the English forces there could be released to support the king's cause in England. Captain Sanford's Company was a part of the contingent landed at Mostyn in November 1643. Hopton commented that these experienced soldiers were 'bold, hardy men, and excellently well officer'd, but the common men verie mutenous and shrewdly infected with rebellious humour of England'. This soldier wears the new coat issued on his arrival in England and carries a 'dog-lock' musket, the 'firelock' which gives the company its name. This type of weapon was usually carried by artillery guards, but several independent companies in the King's Army were wholly equipped with them, examples being Sanford's and Langley's from Ireland and Prince Rupert's 'Firelocks'.

E: Tavern: Colonel Samuel Jones's Regiment, 1643

The most common relaxations of soldiers were drinking, smoking, gambling with cards or dice, and, as some said, quarrelling with one another. They also indulged in some field sports when in camp, such as those described in the ballad *The Gallant She-Soldier*:

> 'For other manly practices she gain's the love of all,
> For leaping and for running or wrestling for a fall,
> For cudgels or for cuffing, if that occasion were,
> There's hardly one of ten men that might
>   with her compare.'

Detail from a portrait of Sir George Wharton, showing a rare contemporary view of Civil War infantry. Note that these musketeers have abandoned their musket rests; and the size of the drum compared with the drummer. The portrait shows these infantry in coats of several different colours. (National Army Museum)

In the absence of barracks soldiers were usually quartered in private houses or barns, the owners being responsible for supplying them with food and drink. Even when provisions were paid for soldiers made poor guests, as can be seen from the comments of one involuntary host: 'My House is, and hath been full of soldiers this fortnight, such uncivil drinkers and thirsty souls that a barrel of good beer trembles at the sight of them and the whole house is nothing but a rendezvous of tobacco and spitting'. Soldiers in garrisons were usually better behaved than those in the marching armies, since they were often local men, and it was easier to obtain justice for misdemeanours. This plate shows Parliament soldiers of Colonel Samuel Jones's Regiment carousing in a tavern in Farnham, where they garrisoned the castle and town.

E1: Fifer

The only musicians on the official establishment of an infantry regiment were the two drummers allowed for each company. It is clear from contemporary references and illustrations, however, that both fifers and drummers were to be found in some units. Sir James Turner's comment 'any Captain may keep a Piper [Fifer] in his Company, and maintain him too, for no pay is allowed him', may explain the absence of these musicians on surviving muster-rolls. This man stands playing in a posture seen in several contemporary illustrations. Note the broad silver trim to his coat, and the cylindrical fife-case slung on its own shoulder belt.

E2: Musketeer
E3: Pikeman

Two soldiers from the garrison, one wearing the regimental green coat while the other has cast his aside as he concentrates on his cards. Samuel Jones's Regiment was typical of those which served in garrison but contributed companies or commanded bodies from time to time for service with the Marching Armies. These regiments kept up their strength better than most, as they were better able to recruit, and fewer of their men deserted or died of the camp sicknesses endemic in the field. The rust stains seen on the coat worn by E3 show him to be a pikeman who usually wears armour.

F: Skirmish: The Westminster Trained Bands at Basing House, 1643

In order to achieve the best effect from the slow rate of fire of the matchlock musket, musketeers were formed into bodies six or eight deep. Each rank would then fire in succession in one of several precise manoeuvres. In some of these the body would stand its ground while firing, in some it would advance, and in others it would retire. This was the Dutch style most commonly used by Parliament troops at the outbreak of the Civil War. In this way well-drilled infantry could keep up a continuous fire, but the emphasis here is on 'well-drilled'—and this scene shows the unfortunate experience of the

An example of a Civil War secret code. These were basically simple, with particular numbers representing individuals, places and articles such as men, money and munitions. Other numbers represent each letter of the alphabet. This code was used in correspondence between Lord Digby and the Parliamentarian Major-General Richard Browne.

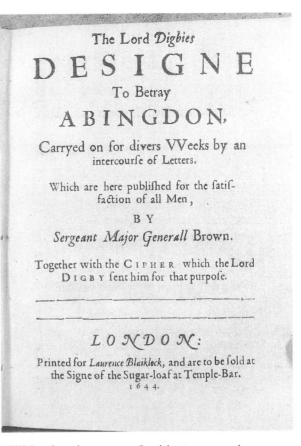

The Lord *Digbies*
DESIGNE
To Betray
ABINGDON,
Carryed on for divers VVeeks by an intercourse of Letters.

Which are here published for the satisfaction of all Men,

BY

Sergeant Major Generall Brown.

Together with the CIPHER which the Lord DIGBY sent him for that purpose.

LONDON:

Printed for *Laurence Blaiklock,* and are to be sold at the Signe of the Sugar-loaf at Temple-Bar.
1644.

A 'Lively Portraiture' of Sergeant-Major-General Richard Browne, and the first page of a pamphlet he had printed in London. The objective was to explain the purpose of his correspondence with the Royalist George, Lord Digby before accusations of treachery could be levelled against him.

Westminster Trained Bands, whose level of training at this point left something to be desired. Lieutenant Elias Archer, who served at the siege, described the catastrophe: 'Whether the fault were in their chiefe Leader, at that present either through want of courage or discretion I know not, but their Front fired before it was possible they could doe any execution, and for want of intervals to turn away speedily the second and third wranks, fired upon them, and so consequently the Reare fired upon their owne Front, and slew or wounded many of their owne men. . . it was told me by a Captain in that Regement, that they had seventy or eighty men slaine or hurt in that disorder'.

In general Trained Bands were regarded as unreliable by both sides as they refused to serve outside their county boundaries, those of London and its suburbs being an exception. London was far too important politically for Parliament to risk offending the City by disarming its Militia and, fortunately for the Parliament cause, the Common Council of the City managed to persuade the

Militia that it was preferable to campaign away from London than at its gates. The soldiers illustrated here are typical of those who fought in a series of campaigns in southern England in 1643 and 1644 with the armies of the Earl of Essex and Sir William Waller.

F1: Officer
This man wears a gold-stitched buff coat over his civilian clothes and lets fall the elaborate 'leading-staff' which is his symbol of rank as he realises that his orders will cause the loss of so many of his men. He wears an orange sash which indicates his allegiance to the Earl of Essex as his general. Since the withdrawal of Sir William Waller's independent commission on 9 October his officers would wear Essex's colours.

F2: Ensign
This officer has the duty of preserving his company's ensign, if necessary at the cost of his own life. He wears blackened armour over his buff coat. Note the dent in his breastplate: the armourer who made it would claim this was the result of firing a

'The Declaration of the Army'. This famous pamphlet contains the declaration addressed to Skippon, Cromwell, Ireton and Fleetwood by 'The Officers of the Army now convened at [Saffron] Waldon'. The soldiers sought satisfaction of their arrears of pay on disbandment, and indemnity for the civil crimes they had committed during the war.

pistol at it to prove its strength, but it was in fact usually made with a chisel as a 'sales pitch'.

F3, 4, 5, 6 Trained Band Musketeers

These soldiers were obliged by statute provide themselves with military equipment, either as musketeers or pikemen, for service in defence of the realm. They wore their own civilian clothes, not uniforms, but contemporary references show that it was the common practice of Trained Band musketeers from London and its suburbs to wear buff-coats as additional protection. To judge from contemporary illustrations these were sleeveless, thinner and cheaper than the heavy sleeved coats worn by cavalry tropers.

As they were responsible for buying their own equipment, sometimes as cheaply as possible, Trained Band soldiers always carried a wide variety of equipment. Each of these men carries a musket heavy enough to require a rest. Although still part of the statutory requirement for a musketeer, only F3 wears a helmet—most musketeers had abandoned its use in the field. Note particularly the unusual covered bandoleer (based on an example in the Tower Armouries) worn by F5; this was an experiment in providing some protection from the weather for the powder containers, but as there is no evidence that it was ever a military issue it was probably custom built for a Militia soldier.

G: Encampment: Army of the Solemn League and Covenant, 1644

On 27 September 1643 an alliance termed the Solemn League and Covenant was signed in Westminster by members of both Houses of Parliament and a group of Commissioners from Scotland. This document contained both civil and religious clauses and the price of Scottish military aid was the supremacy of the Presbyterian discipline in England, Scotland and Ireland. The rather loose phrasing of this document left plenty of room for debate in the future and the Scots later accused the English of deceiving them. In reality, however, this was an alliance of necessity, not conviction, as the king's cause was then in the ascendant and neither Parliament nor the Scots could afford to see King Charles triumphant. The Scots commander, the Earl of Leven, crossed the Tweed into England on 19 January 1644 with an army of 19 regiments of foot, nine of horse and one of dragoons.

As might be expected, elaborate arrangements were made for the religious well-being of this army, with morning and evening prayers and sermons on Sundays, in emulation of the godly army of the Swedish champion Gustavus Adolphus. In the event, however, few ministers could be persuaded to follow the army to England, and it fell away from the high standards of the Scots army during the Bishops' Wars. This group of soldiers are unlucky to have been surprised playing dice on the Sabbath by a minister zealous enough to stay with the army.

G1: Sergeant

Large numbers of Scots has served as mercenaries during the Thirty Years' War in Europe, particularly in the Swedish army, and many returned home once a native Scots army was formed. This made it an unusually professional force; although the colonels and the captains of companies were men of local standing but little experience, the lieutenant-colonels and majors were usually all professionals. Like many of his colleagues this professional wears a buff-coat and a gorget for protection; and the halberd he carries is an indication of his rank.

G2: Musketeer
G3: Musketeer
Scots infantry were distinguished by the 'hodden-grey' coats they wore and their blue bonnets, so much so that at the siege of Carlisle 'one died in ye towne, who wereing a blue cap wych he had taken from ye Scotch at Stannix, was mistaken in ye last action at Denton House, received his death wound by Richard Grave, a Cavalier'. One soldier has put his 'Swedish feather', on the ground beside him; this was simply a short stake topped with a pike-head which was set in front of a line of musketeers as an additional defence against cavalry, and as the name suggests it was used in the Swedish army in which so many Scots served. The Scots are the only troops known to have been issued with these stakes during the Civil War, but it is uncertain whether they ever used them in action. Scots pikemen were not issued with armour. This may have been because of the influence of professional soldiers with experience of the European wars in which armour had largely been abandoned to achieve swifter marches, or it may simply have been an example of Scots economy.

G4: Presbyterian Minister
A number of ministers had accompanied the Scots army during the Bishops' Wars and, as Robert Baillie recalled of its encampment, 'Had ye lent your ear in the morning, or especially at even, and heard in the tents the sound of some singing psalms, some praying, and some reading Scripture, ye would have been refreshed'. Few, however, were prepared to march with the army into England, or to stay long if they did, so that in April 1645 'in two and twenty regiments there is not one Minister'. The danger from the Scots' point of view was that the lack of religious fellowship led to a breakdown of

discipline as professional officers introduced the habits they had picked up in the vicious European wars. Worse than this from a Presbyterian point of view was the possibility of Independents of the Earl of Manchester's Army corrupting 'our simple silly lads'.

H: Battle: The New Model Army, Naseby 1645
This scene shows the closing stages of the Battle of Naseby as Parliament's New Model Army overran the last of the infantry of the King's Oxford Army. The campaigns of 1644 had shown that by combining several of its regional armies, Parliament could achieve a significant numerical advantage over the King's forces, but divided command and internal rivalries prevented its exploitation. The New Model Army shared the equipment and theoretical unit organisation of its predecessors but it had a unified command, strongly-recruited

'A Representation from His Excellency Sir Thomas Fairfax': another expression of the 'Desires of the Army', setting out their conditions for disbandment. By September 1647 both officers and men were united in their demands.

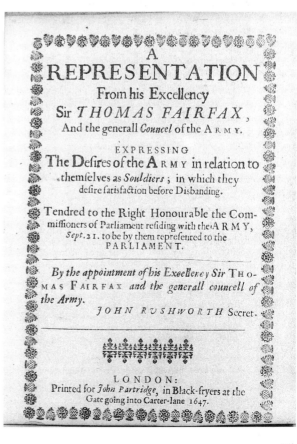

A
REPRESENTATION
From his Excellency
Sir *THOMAS FAIRFAX*,
And the generall *Councel* of the ARMY.

EXPRESSING
The Desires of the ARMY in relation to
themselves as *Souldiers*; in which they
desire satisfaction before Disbanding.

Tendred to the Right Honourable the Commissioners of Parliament residing with the ARMY, *Sept. 21.* to be by them represented to the PARLIAMENT.

By the appointment of his Excellency Sir THOMAS FAIRFAX *and the generall councell of the Army.*
JOHN RUSHWORTH Secret.

LONDON:
Printed for *John Partridge*, in Black-fryers at the Gate going into Carter-lane 1647.

regiments, and an adequate pay-chest. This was the key to its success.

The appearance of the New Model Army was different, as for the first time each regiment in the Army was issued with coats of a uniform colour. The newspaper *Perfect Passages* for 7 May 1645 records 'the men are redcoats all, the whole army only are distinguished by several facings of their coats', facings being the lining of the coat which showed where it was turned back at the cuffs. Their discipline had not yet reached the high level for which the New Model Army became famous; as Sir Samuel Luke wrote on 10 June 1645 of those he saw: 'I think all these New Modellers knead all their dough with ale, for I never saw so many drunk in my life in so short a time. The men I have formerly wrote to you are extraordinarily personable, well armed and well-paid, but the officers you will hardly distinguish from common soldiers'.

Sir Thomas Fairfax, commander of the cavalry of his father Ferdinando, Lord Fairfax's Northern Army, and later commander of the New Model Army. An intensely fair-minded man, he stood by his soldiers in their mutiny for fair conditions on disbandment, but refused to sign the king's death warrant. (David Carter collection)

H1, H2: *Pikeman and Musketeer, Sir Thomas Fairfax's Regiment of Foot*

Both wear the New Model's red coat with the blue linings and ties which distinguish this regiment from its fellows. The pikeman retains the back and breast plates of his armour, but has discarded the gorget and tassets. The pikemen in some regiments may have wholly abandond their armour by this time, although all retained their helmets. The musketeer carries the latest light-pattern musket and has discarded his musket-rest. One distinctive piece of equipment was the bandoleer specified in contract books for the New Model, which was 'to bee of wood with whole bottoms, to be turned within and not Bored, the Heads to be of Wood, and to be layd in oyle (vizt) Three times over, and to be coloured blew with blew and white strings with strong thred twist with good belts, att Twenty pence a peece'.

H3: *Ensign, Prince Rupert's Regiment of Foot*

King Charles also made efforts to 'new-model' his Oxford-based army in 1644, but the fixed interests of his officers defeated him and the large number of weak units with their large and expensive officer corps remained. This did not detract from their fighting quality, and the King's infantry performed better than the numerically superior New Model at Naseby; but they were far more expensive to maintain than similar numbers of Parliament foot soldiers. The king's failure was an illustration of his weak overall control of his army, whose increasing indiscipline made them, and by implication his own cause, ever more obnoxious in the provinces.

Prince Rupert's Regiment was one of the best units in King Charles's Oxford Army; first raised by Sir Thomas Lunsford in 1642, it was later commanded by his brother Henry, who fell at the storm of Bristol, and then became Prince Rupert's. Actual command was exercised by Lieutenant-Colonel John Russell. Despite the severe casualties it must have suffered at Marston Moor, the regiment still numbered some 500 men at Naseby, possibly the strongest Royalist regiment in the field—a recruiting effort that is a tribute to the charisma of its Colonel. At least four of the regiment's ensigns were captured at Naseby, and subsequently seen in London and recorded by the contemporary artist Jonathan Turmile. The ensign shown was probably the second captain's.

I: Aftermath: Marston Moor 1644

This plate shows a scene following the Battle of Marston Moor in which Prince Rupert's Army and the Marquis of Newcastle's Northern (Royalist) Army were destroyed. The last stage in this series of views of the life of the soldier is the surgeon's attention. A pikeman from the Marquis of Newcastle's Regiment sits in his shirtsleeves as a surgeon probes the wound in his chest; a musketeer from the Earl of Manchester's Regiment holds him steady.

I1: Pikeman, Marquis of Newcastle's Regiment

Newcastle was appointed General of the King's Forces north of the Trent at the outbreak of the war and used his considerable local influence to raise an army for the king's cause. His forces managed to gain the upper hand over the Parliamentarian Fairfaxes in 1643, but the entry of the Earl of Leven's Scottish army the following year upset the balance of power, and the junction of the Scots army, Fairfax's Northern Parliament troops and the Army of the Eastern Association proved too much for him. His infantry were commonly known as 'Whitecoats', a reference to the undyed cloth used to make their coats. One Parliament newsheet suggests that in some cases the coats were decorated with crosses, 'an Ensigne wee conceive of some Popish Regiment'. While Newcastle emigrated after the battle rather than 'endure the laughter of the Court', his regiment was steadfast: 'Having got into a small parcel of ground ditched in, and not of easy access of horse, would take no quarter, and by mere valour for one whole hour kept the troops of horse from entering them at near push of Pike . . . they would have no quarter but fought it out until there was not thirty of them living'.

I2: Musketeer, Earl of Manchester's Regiment

Manchester's infantry consisted of 11 regiments in all, four for garrison duty in the Eastern Association counties and seven for field service. He brought six to fight at Marston Moor, one being his own green-coated regiment. Two of the other regiments in the Eastern Association, Thomas Rainsborough's and Edward Montagu's, are known to have worn red coats but those of the other regiments are unknown. It is possible that the bulk of Manchester's infantry wore red coats, but the *Newes sent by Mr. Ogden*

Charles I: King of England, Scotland and Ireland, he experienced revolutions in all three. A firm believer in the 'Divine Right of Kings', he considered it excused any treachery in maintaining his position. His incompetence as a conspirator alienated all parties, and a major reason for his execution was that his promises for future arrangements could not be trusted. (David Carter collection)

following Marston Moor includes the comment 'most of Manchesters base blew coats which fought under the bloody colors are cutt off', which indicates that some infantry other than his personal regiment did not. Note the musket left propped in its rest, the common way of stacking arms at the time.

I3: Surgeon

The medical services of this period can best be described as desperately inadequate. Armies on both sides usually had two or three 'Physicians General' attached to headquarters, and each regiment had a chirurgeon and two mates on its staff. The demands on these few men after a battle

Edward Earl of CLARENDON Lord High CHANCELLOR of England and Chancellor of the University of Oxford An° Dom 1667

A strong believer in the English Constitution, Edward Hyde was a firm supporter of Charles I during the Civil War, and of his son thereafter. He became Lord Chancellor on the Restoration. The illustration is from his famous *History of the Rebellion*.

can be imagined. Note the surgeon's tools laid out in front of his chest.

J: Musketeers' equipment
J1: Musketeers

A front and back view of typical musketeers showing how the equipment was worn. In order to achieve a reasonable rate of fire musketeers were taught to load and fire according to a very precise series of movements or 'Postures', the object being that by practising the sequence over and over the soldier would become steadily more expert, and more of a danger to his enemies than his friends. Different manuals had different numbers of postures for this process, sometimes up to 60; but this was only for training, and in action the orders were reduced to three, 'Make Ready; Present; Give Fire'. The two postures seen here are 'Charge with Powder' and 'Poyse your Musket'.

J2: Hats and Montero caps

According to military theorists musketeers should wear helmets as part of their equipment, and the specifications for the Trained Bands still included a helmet. In practice few musketeers in professional service still did, the Dutch being the only significant exception. Instead musketeers wore a variety of broad-brimmed hats or peaked Montero caps such as those shown here.

J3 and J4: Bandoleers

The bandoleer was a leather belt to which 12 or more wooden containers were strung, each containing enough coarse gunpowder to fire a single round. At its base was a pouch in which musket balls and cleaning equipment were kept; and suspended beneath it was a flask containing fine powder to prime the musket. The small metal container seen on J4 contained oil. The unusual bandoleer shown in J3 is an experimental style with a leather flap to keep the powder containers dry, possibly produced for a Militia enthusiast. The containers surrounding show some of the styles used. The instruments shown are a match-cover, sometimes used to protect one end of the matchcord from the elements; a worm, and a scourer. Both of the last two had a screw thread at the base which fitted into the rear end of the ramrod; the first was used to draw out a charge which had not gone off, and the second to clean out the barrel itself.

J5: Muskets

The majority of muskets used during the Civil War were matchlocks, that is to say they were fired by bringing a length of smouldering matchcord into contact with powder in the priming pan. One major development was the introduction of a new lighter pattern. This had a shorter barrel, and a slimmer, lighter stock. Musketeers using this lighter pattern could dispense with their forked musket-rests, but

Sir John Hotham, whose refusal to deliver Hull and the powerful arsenal stored there was a critical blow to the king's cause at the outbreak of the war. He and his son later had second thoughts and offered to deliver Hull to the king; the plot was discovered, and both father and son were executed as a result. (David Carter collection)

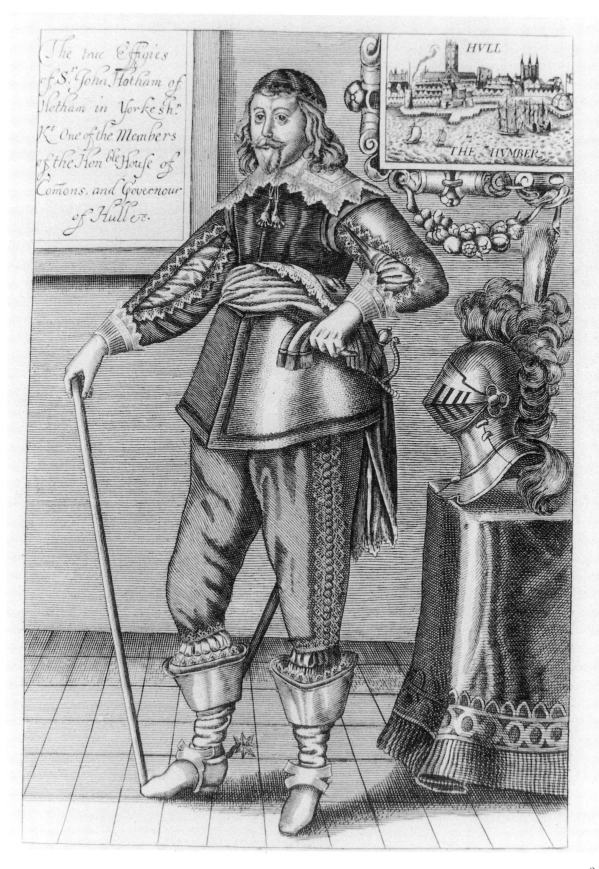

The true Effigies
of Sr. John Hotham of
Hotham in Yorkesh.r
Kt. One of the Members
of the Honble House of
Comons, and Governour
of Hull &c.

HVLL

THE HVMBER

61

Sᵣ John Meldrum

Sir John Meldrum, a Scots professional soldier and an asset to the Parliamentary cause, serving at Edgehill and commanding at the unsuccessful siege of Newark. He was killed at the siege of Scarborough during a sally by the defenders.

Edward Massey Esqʳ. Major Generall of the west

Edward Massey, famous for his truly heroic defence of Gloucester against the King's Army. He was involved in efforts to oppose the New Model Army after the Civil War, and was forced to flee to Holland. He later became a supporter of Charles II.

any who had the older style could not. Examples of both styles are shown.

K: Pikemen's equipment
The combination of Pikemen and Musketeers was necessary because without the defence provided by Pikemen, infantry could be ridden into the ground by a cavalry attack.

K1: Pikemen
A front and back view of typical pikemen. As with musketeers, there was a precise series of 'Postures' for the pike, although there were fewer of them. The importance of the drill becomes obvious when one considers a large body of pikemen carrying 16-foot pikes with only three feet between one man and the next: unless each man went through the same series of movements at the same time chaos followed. The postures shown here are 'Advance Your Pike', and 'Charge to ye Reare' (second motion).

K2: Helmets and Monmouth caps
With the outbreak of the Civil War obsolete equipment which had been stored in the Tower of London or private armouries was brought into service together with more modern patterns. The seizure of Trained Band arsenals must also have contributed some quite ancient models. Those shown in the top row date from the 16th century, while those in the second are patterns know to have been issued in the 17th. Two views of the woollen Monmouth cap commonly worn by pikemen for padding under their helmets are shown in the second row; the first shows the appearance of the cap and the second how it was worn with the brim up.

K3: Armour and pike-heads
A complete set of pikeman's armour consisted of a

gorget back, breast and tassets. This was the specification for the Militia and the Muster Master would have checked that all was present before a Trained Band pikeman 'passed muster'. Professional soldiers tended to lighten the load by abandoning the gorget and, sometimes, the tassets. In the years following the Civil War the New Model Army abandoned the use of armour altogether. The head of the pike was to be 'well steeled, eight inches long, well-riveted, the butt end bound with a ring of iron'.

K4 & K5: Rapiers, backswords and other patterns
Most infantrymen, whether musketeers or pikemen, were issued with swords of one pattern or another. The examples shown here are popular styles, including the simple cross-hilt seen in several contemporary illustrations. General Monk thought this a waste of time, advising the issue of 'a good stiff Tuck not very long, with a Belt, for if you arm your men with Swords, half the Swords you have in your Army amongst your common men, will be upon the first March you make be broken with cutting of boughs'. No doubt he spoke from bitter experience.

Notes sur les planches en couleur

A: Gentilhommes d'une association de volontaires se réunissant pour s'entraîner, pour des raisons plus mondaines que militaires. **A1:** Ce 'soldat doublement armé' est né de l'idée d'associer l'arme nationale—l'arc—à la pique; il n'existe pas de témoignage que ce fut jamais employé en bataille. **A2:** L'équipement complet du piquier, tel que stipulé par la loi pour la milice. Les hommes moins fortunés noircissaient ou enduisaient de brun leur armure pour l'empêcher de rouiller. **A3:** A nouveau, équipement réglementaire complet, mais d'une richesse peu courante.

B1: Clerc de la compagnie inscrivant le détail d'une recrue; il porte des vêtements civils, comme tous les officiers de cette époque. **B2:** Officier du King's Lifeguard of Foot, son rang se voit à sa pertuisane et son allégeance au roi à sa ceinture rouge. La seule autre pièce militaire montrée ici est le gorgerin. **B3:** Les tambours, au nombre de deux par compagnie, portaient le costume que leurs officiers avaient conçu (et payé) pour eux.

C: Des troupes parlementaires pillant une demeure catholique au début de la guerre; la discipline fut améliorée à compter de 1645. **C1:** Chaque recrue était censée recevoir un pourpoint, une chemise, des chaussrues, une casquette et une musette, quoique par 'casquette' l'on entendait tous genres de coiffures. Ce soldat, en pourpoint vert doublé de jaune de son régiment, porte une casquette 'Montero'. **C2:** Un autre mousquetaire, avec le pourpoint jaune de son régiment et un chapeau en feutre à bords larges. Sa bandoulière est d'un modèle différent et son épée plus moderne que celle de son compagnon. **C3:** Les bonnets de laine 'Monmouth' étaient populaires chez les piquiers, et lui servaient de bourre sous leur casque. Il porte son armure noircie contre la rouille sur le pourpoint rouge de son régiment.

D1: Seul le ruban rouge de son bonnet le distingue d'un civil. Son vieux mousquet, lourd demande à être appuyé sur une fourche. **D2:** Il porte les cartouches de son mousquet plus léger dans un sac en cuir huilé. Le pourpoint, les culottes et la casquette 'Montero' proviennent des stocks fournis à cette armée par le marchand Bushell; les ensembles de l'habit étaient ou tout en rouge, ou tout en bleu. **D3** Les mousquets à pierre étaient principalement utilisés par les gardes d'artillerie, mais cette compagnie endurcie et fraiche revenue de sa campagne d'Irlande faisait partie des quelques unités d'infanterie indépendantes qui les aient reçus.

E1 Les fifres n'étaient pas sur la liste officielle des effectifs de l'unité mais étaient payés par les officiers. **E2, E3:** L'un porte le pourpoint vert du régiment—les tâches de rouille suggèrent qu'il fut piquier et portait normalement son armure au-dessus de son pourpoint. Cette unité a servi dans la garnison de Farnham; les hommes faisaient attention à mieux se comporter dans les tavernes locales que les soldats qui traversaient simplement la ville.

F: Pendant la bataille qui eut lieu à ce manoir assiégé, le manque d'expérience conduisit des rangées successives de cette unité de milice à tirer dans le dos de leurs compagnons en position avancée. **F1:** Tenue caractéristique dénotant la qualité d'officier, avec buff-coat à point d'or, ceinture orange montrant son allégeance au Comte d'Essex et 'leading-staff' ou pertuisane comme marque de range. **F2** L'enseigne porte le drapeau de la compagnie; centre d'attraction de l'attaque ennemie, il est protégé par quelques pièces d'armure. La bosselure sur la plaque de poitrine, marque manifeste qu'elle a été éprouvée par le fabricant en tirant au pistolet sur elle, était, souvent faite au marteau par les fournisseurs malhonnêtes. **F3, 4, 5, 6:** Les soldats de milice des Trained Bands devaient fournir leur propre habit, qui n'était pas uniforme, ainsi que leur équipement et armes qui devaient être conformes à la norme légale; la variété était donc grande. Les unités de Londres semblent avoir eu une prédisposition pour de fins buff-coats sans manche. L'on ne portait pratiquement pas de casque, bien que les instructions officielles continuaient à l'exiger.

Farbtafeln

A: Ehrenmänner einer Freiwilligenvereinigung, die sich zum Exerzieren trafen. Diese Treffen hatten eher einen geselligen als militärischen Charakter.

A1: Dieser 'zweifach bewaffnete Mann' verdeutlicht die Idee, die nataonale Waffe—den Langbogen—mit dem Langspiess (oder der Pike) als Bewaffnung zu kombinieren. Nichts weist jedoch darauf hin, dass diese Waffenkombination jemals in einer Schlacht benutzt wurde. **A2:** Die gesamte Austrüstung eines Pikeniers, die in den gesetzlichen Vorschriften der Bürgerwehr festgelegt worden war. Weniger wohlhabende Männer schwärzten oder bräunten ihre Panzerung, so dass sie nicht rostete. **A3:** Wiederum die volle, gesetzlich vorgeschriebene Austrüstung, die von ungewöhnlichem Reichtum zeugte.

B1: Der Schriftführer der Kompanie trägt Zivilbekleidung—wie es in dieser Zeit bei Offizieren üblich war—und nimmt die Personalien eines Rekruten auf. **B2:** Ein Offizier der King's Lifeguard of Foot. Die Partisane (Stosswaffe) lässt seinen Rang erkennen. Überdies ist der Kragenspiegel hier dargestellt. **B3:** Jede Kompanie hatte zwei Trommler, deren Tracht von ihren Offizieren entworfen und bezahlt wurde.

C: Die Soldaten des Parlamentsheeres plündern das Haus einer katholischen Familie zu Kriegsbeginn. Ab 1645 wurde die Disziplin besser gewahrt.

C1: Angeblich wurde an jeden Rekrut ein Mantel, Hemd, Schuhe, Schirmmütze—dabei konnte es sich um irgend eine Art von Kopfbedeckung handeln—ausgegeben. Dieser Soldat trägt einen grünen Regimentsmantel mit gelbem Futter und einer Montero-Mütze. **C2:** Ein weiterer Musketier mit grauem Regimentsmantel und einem breitkrempigen Filzhut. Das Bandolier birgt ein anderes Muster; sein Schwert ist moderner, als das seines Kameraden. **C3:** Die 'Monmouth'-Mützen waren bei den Pikenieren beliebt und wurden unter dem Helm zum auswattieren getragen. Die Panzerung wurde gegen Rostbildung geschwärzt und über die rote Bekleidung angelegt.

D1: Nur das rote Hutband unterscheidet ihn von einem Zivilisten. Seine alte, schwere Muskete muss auf einer Stütze abgelegt werden. **D2:** Patronen für leichtere Musketen wurden in einer geölten Ledertasche aufbewahrt. Mantel, Breecheshosen und 'Montero'-Mütze stammten aus Armeebeständen, die von 'Bushell'-Kaufleuten zur Verfügung gestellt wurden. Die Bekleidung war entweder in rot oder blau gehalten. **D3:** Steinschloss-Musketen wurden hauptsächlich von den Artilleriegarden benutzt, diese kampferfahrene Kompanie, die gerade aus Irland zurückgekommen war, war nur eine der wenigen, unabhängigen Infanterie-Einheiten, die man damit ausgestattet hatte.

E1: Querpfeifer gehörten nicht zu den offiziellen Einheiten, wurden allerdings von Offizieren bezahlt. **E2, E3:** Eine Person trägt den grünen Regimentsmantel mit rostfarbenen Schmutzflecken, die darauf zurückschliessen, dass es sich um einen Pikenier handelt. In der Regel trugen sie darüber eine Panzerung. Diese Einheit diente in der Farnham Garnison. Die Männer taten ihr Nötigstes, sich in der Stadtschenke besser zu benehmen als die Soldaten, die nur kurz in der Stadt verweilten.

F: Im Laufe der Kampfhandlungen, am besetzten Herrenhaus, führte die Unerfahrenheit verschiedener Bürgerwehren dazu, dass diese in die Rücken ihrer Kameraden schossen.

F1: Die typische Bekleidung eines Qualitätsoffiziers mit goldbesticktem 'Buff-Coat'. Die orangefarbene Schärpe wurde von jenen getragen, die dem Graf von Essex eine Treue geschworen hatten. Das 'Leading-staff' oder die Partisane dienten als Rangabzeichen. **F2:** Der Fähnrich trägt die Kompanieflagge. Da er im Mittelpunkt des feindlichen Angriffs stand, trug er eine Panzerung. Die Beule in der Brustplatte—offensichtlich ein Gütezeichen, welches der Kunsthandwer-

G: L'armée presbytérienne écossaise fut dotée de bien peu de pasteurs à cette occasion—ces soldats ont eu la malchance de se faire prendre. . . **G1:** Le gorgerin et le buff-coat suggèrent qu'il s'agit d'un des nombreux vétérans du service des mercenaires sous Gustavus Adolphus à se trouver dans les rangs écossais; la hallebarde, son grade de sergent. **G2:** Le pourpoint en 'hodden grey' et le béret bleu étaient pratiquement universels parmi les Ecossais. Le pieu ferré, ou 'plume suédoise' ne fut délivré qu'aux troupes écossaises pendant la guerre civile. **G3:** Les piquiers écossais portaient des casques mais pas d'armure, peut-être parce que nombre d'entre eux avaient servi dans des guerres étrangères où cela était passé de mode. **G4:** Pasteur, dans un costume caractéristique de sa vocation et de l'époque.

H1, H2: Piquier et mousquetaire du Fairfax's Regiment portaient des pourpoints rouges délivrés à toute l'armée—pour la toute première fois—en 1645, les régiments se distinguaient par la couleur de leurs doublures. Ce premier a ôté son gorgerin et ses tassettes. Ce dernier porte un mousquet léger, qui ne demande pas de fourche, et une bandoulière conforme à la description donnée en grands détails dans les contrats de l'armée. **H3:** Bien qu'alors relativement affaibli, ce régiment royaliste a combattu avec grande force d'esprit à Naseby; mais quatre de ses drapeaux furent capturés—cet exemple est probablement celui du Second Capitaine de la Compagnie.

I1: Le 'Newcastle Whitecoats' s'est battu pratiquement jusqu'au dernier homme à Marston Moor. **I2:** Le Manchester's Regiment portait des pourpoints verts. Notez le mousquet et sa fourche calés ensemble selon l'usage. **I3:** Les chirurgiens portaient des vêtements civils.

J1: Les très nombreux mouvements présentés dans les livres d'exercice de l'époque étaient conçus pour l'entrainement; bien moins d'ordres étaient donnés en bataille. **J2:** Des chapeaux à bords larges et des casquettes 'Montero' que portaient les mousquetaires. **J3, J4:** Plusieurs bandoulières, avec des sacs à balles, de petites fioles d'une poudre d'amorce plus fine et une bouteille métallique d'huile. Vous pouvez également voir ici un couvre-mèche, un 'worm' pour retirer les charges qui n'ont pas été tirées, et un écouvillon pour nettoyer le canon—ces deux outils se vissaient sur la baguette. **J5:** Toute une variété de mousquets légers et lourds.

K1: Des piquiers dans deux positions d'exercice; un entrainement précis était évidemment important pour les hommes qui portaient de longues piques en rangs serrés. **K2:** Casques et bonnets de laine 'Monmouth' que portaient les piquiers. **K3:** Armure et têtes de piques. **K4, K5:** Des épées de modèles divers.

ker mit einer Pistole angebracht hatte; unehrliche Handwerker benutzten dazu einen Hammer. **F3, 4, 5, 6:** Die Männer der Bürgerwehr aus der 'Trained Bands' mussten ihre eigene Bekleidung zur Verfügung stellen, die uneinheitlich und vorschriftsmässig nicht festgelegt war. Dies erklärt die grossen Unterschiede. Die Londoner Einheiten bevorzugten wohl die dünnen, ärmellosen 'Buff-Coats'. Helme wurden selten getragen, obgleich die Vorschrift dies verlangte.

G: Die schottische presbyterianische Armee war zu diesem Aufeinandertreffen nicht ausreichend mit Geistlichen versorgt. Diese Männer hatten kein Glück—sie wurden gefangengenommen.

G1: Der Kragenspiel und 'Buff-Coat' lässt darauf schliessen, dass einer der vielen Veteranen aus dem besoldeten Heer des Gustavus Adolphus stammte, die sich nun in den schottischen Rängen wiederfanden. Die Hellbarde verdeutlicht seinen Rang. **G2:** Der Mantel aus grobem, ungefärbtem Wollstoff (hodden grey) und die blaue Baskenmütze wurde nahezu von allen Schotten getragen. Der mit Eisen beschlagene Pfahl oder die 'schwedische Feder' wurden nur an die schottischen Soldaten im Bürgerkrieg ausgegeben. **G3:** Schottische Pikeniere trugen Helme, aber keine Panzerung. Dies ist vielleicht darauf zurückzuführen, dass viele von ihnen in ausländischen Kriegen mitgewirkt hatten, wo dies nicht mehr üblich war. **G4:** Ein Geistlicher in der typischen Tracht, die seiner Berufung und der Zeit entsprach.

H1, H2: Pikeniere und Musketiere des 'Fairfax's Regiment' trugen die roten Mäntel, die von der gesamten Armee verwendet wurden. Im Jahre 1645 unterschieden sich die Regimenter zum ersten Mal durch das farbige Innenfutter. Die vorher erwähnten, benutzten nicht mehr die Kragenspiegel und Quasten. Der letztgenannte hat eine leichte Muskete, die nicht auf einer Stütze abgelegt werden muss und einen Patronengurt, der ausführlich in den Armeeverträgen beschrieben wurde.

H3: Obgleich das königliche Regiment schon verhältnismässig geschwächt worden war, fochten sie mit unerbittlichem Kampfgeist in Naseby. Dennoch wurden vier ihrer Flaggen erbeutet. Die abgebildete Fahne gehörte wahrscheinlich dem Zweiten Kapitän der Kompanie.

I1: Die 'Newcastle's Whitecoats' kämpften bis zum bitteren Ende im Marston Moor. **I2:** Das Manchester Regiment war in grüne Mäntel gekleidet. Beachtenswert ist die Muskete und die normal aufgestellte Stütze. **I3:** Chirurgen trugen Zivilbekleidung.

J1: Die zahlreichen Stellungen, die in den Übungsbüchern abgebildet sind, dienten Ausbildungszwecken. Während der Kampfhandlungen wurden weitaus weniger Befehle gegeben. **J2:** Breitkrempige Hüte und Montero-Mützen, die von den Musketieren getragen wurden. **J3, J4:** Unterschiedliche Patronengurte mit Munitionstaschen, kleinen Flaschen mit feingemahlenem Zündpulver sowie eine metallene Ölflasche. Ebenso abgebildet ist ein Zündholzbehälter, ein 'Worm' um nicht explodierte Geschosse zu entfernen und ein Reinigungsstab—diese beiden Werkzeuge konnten auf den Ladestock geschraubt werden. **J5:** Verschiedene— leichte und schwere—Musketen.

K1: Pikeniere in zwei Übungsstellungen. Gute Ausbildung war offensichtlich von grösster Bedeutung für diejenigen, die die Langspiesse in engen Mannschaftsgruppierungen mit sich führten. **K2:** Helme und Monmouth-Mützen, die von den Pikenieren getragen wurden. **K3:** Panzerung und Hakenspitzen. **K4, K5:** Unterschiedliche Schwerter.